Excellence for all **children**
Meeting Special Educational Needs

Presented to Parliament by
the Secretary of State for Education and Employment
by Command of Her Majesty

October 1997

CM 3785

WP 2110742 4

£11.90

CONTENTS

Please note that all statistics quoted for January 1997 are provisional figures derived from the Schools' Census (Form 7).

Foreword

by the Secretary of State for Education and Employment, the Rt Hon David Blunkett MP

There is nothing more important to the Government than raising the standards children achieve in our schools. The White Paper **Excellence in schools** committed us to exacting targets, and proposed a challenging programme to achieve them.

Our vision is of excellence for all. This inclusive vision encompasses children with special educational needs (SEN). Schools currently identify 18% of children as having special educational needs of differing kinds. Almost 3% have individual statements showing the additional special educational provision they require. This Green Paper asks some questions about these figures. What is not in question is the case for setting our sights high for all these children.

Good provision for SEN does not mean a sympathetic acceptance of low achievement. It means a tough-minded determination to show that children with SEN are capable of excellence. Where schools respond in this way, teachers sharpen their ability to set high standards for *all* pupils.

The great majority of children with SEN will, as adults, contribute economically; all will contribute as members of society. Schools have to prepare all children for these roles. That is a strong reason for educating children with SEN, as far as possible, with their peers. Where all children are included as equal partners in the school community, the benefits are felt by all. That is why we are committed to comprehensive and enforceable civil rights for disabled people. Our aspirations as a nation must be for all our people.

Our approach to improving the achievement of children with special educational needs has six themes:

- our high expectations for all children include <u>high expectations for children with SEN</u>. All our programmes for raising standards will reflect this, starting from pre-school provision, building on the information provided by the new arrangements for baseline assessment when children start in primary school, and leading to improved ways of tackling problems with early literacy and numeracy;

- while recognising the paramount importance of meeting the needs of individual children, and the necessity of specialist provision for some, we shall promote the <u>inclusion of children with SEN within mainstream schooling</u> wherever possible. We shall remove barriers which get in the way of meeting the needs of all children and redefine the role of special schools to develop a network of specialist support. We attach high priority to the development of new regional arrangements for improving the effectiveness of SEN provision;

- we want <u>all parents of children with SEN</u> to get effective support from the full range of local services and voluntary agencies, to have a real say in decisions about their child's education, and to be empowered to contribute themselves to their child's development. Some parents need to be helped to gain access to these opportunities;

- we want good value for money from the one-seventh of their budget – £2.5 billion – which local education authorities (LEAs) currently spend on special educational needs. This is not about cost-cutting. It is about ensuring that this provision leads to achievement at school, and success in adult life. We want to look at ways of <u>shifting resources</u> from expensive remediation to cost-effective prevention and early intervention; to shift the emphasis from <u>procedures to practical support</u>; and to see whether changes should be made to any aspects of statements of SEN;

- we shall <u>boost opportunities for staff development</u> in SEN, and see that good practice is widely disseminated, so that the principles of this Green Paper can be put into practice;

- we know that positive approaches to special needs make a difference. We shall work in co-operation with all who share our objective of high standards for children with SEN; and we shall expect provision locally to be based on a <u>partnership of all those with a contribution to make.</u>

This Green Paper is the first step in a fundamental reappraisal of the way we meet special educational needs. It explains our approach. It challenges some widespread assumptions. Above all, it seeks the views of all those with an interest in special educational needs on how to make a reality of our vision. The Paper includes examples to show what is currently being achieved. These are not intended as benchmarks of best practice but to demonstrate good practice on which we can build.

We have set up a National Advisory Group on SEN, chaired by the Minister responsible for SEN, Estelle Morris MP. This Group, whose membership is listed in Appendix 1, has been influential in the preparation of this Green Paper. It will work closely with our Standards Task Force. Members of the Group will play an important part in the arrangements for consultation on the Green Paper.

This consultation process will include conferences, meetings and discussions throughout the country. Many organisations have already announced their intention to contribute actively to this debate. I hope that there will be much local discussion. A copy of the Green Paper is being sent to all headteachers, chairs of governing bodies, SEN co-ordinators and LEAs. A summary leaflet will also be made available.

Early in 1998, the National Advisory Group on SEN will consider the results of this consultation, and will advise the Government on a programme to drive forward improvements. After that, if there is a need to change the law, we will seek an early opportunity to do so. While there is much scope for more effective targeting of expenditure within the large SEN budget, we know that there will be transitional costs in implementing our programme. The pace of change will be linked to the availability of resources. Action will be carefully phased, bearing in mind everything that is being asked of schools and LEAs. Our objective is a programme for this Parliament and beyond, sustaining high quality provision for children with special educational needs well into the twenty first century.

David Blunkett

A programme for early action…

The following section summarises what we aim to achieve for SEN provision over the lifetime of this Parliament. Much of that programme will depend on the responses to this Green Paper. But we want to make urgent progress in key areas, to help prepare for action in all parts of the country and in all schools over the next few years. We are therefore announcing a series of co-ordinated projects to kick start the process. By early next year, each of the actions described below will be under way.

- We shall be working with a group of LEAs and schools with relevant experience, to establish the necessary conditions for promoting inclusion much more widely.

- We shall be working with schools in a small number of LEAs, to find ways in which staff in special and mainstream schools can most effectively support each other.

- We shall be funding research to assess the relative costs, benefits and practical implications of educating children in mainstream and special schools.

- We shall announce a significant expansion in the Schools Access Initiative, to help mainstream schools become more accessible to children with disabilities.

- We shall be supporting projects in two regional Government Offices, to prepare for the introduction of regional planning arrangements for SEN.

- We shall be working with a group of LEAs, schools and voluntary bodies representing parents, to promote effective arrangements for parent partnership.

- We shall be supporting a project to help special schools develop procedures for target setting.

- The DfEE, with the support of OFSTED, will run a programme of practical workshops to help special schools for children with emotional and behavioural difficulties improve the achievement of their pupils.

- All Government policies for schools will include an explicit assessment of the implications for children with special educational needs.

By 2002...

At the end of each chapter is a summary of what we aim to achieve for children with special educational needs over the lifetime of this Parliament. All the summaries are brought together here.

By 2002...

1

- The policies set out in *Excellence in schools* for raising standards, particularly in the early years, will be beginning to reduce the number of children who need long-term special educational provision.

- There will be stronger and more consistent arrangements in place across the country for the early identification of SEN.

- Schools and parents will have higher expectations of the standards children with SEN can attain.

- Target setting, in both mainstream and special schools, will take explicit account of the scope for improving the achievements of children with special educational needs.

- New Entry Level awards will be available for pupils for whom GNVQs or GCSEs at 16 are not appropriate.

- There will be more effective and widespread use of Information and Communications Technology to support the education of children with SEN, in both mainstream and special schools.

By 2002...

2

- All parents whose children are being assessed for a statement of SEN will be offered the support of an independent "Named Person".

- Parent partnership schemes will be in place in every LEA in England, and will play an important part in supporting parents of children with SEN.

- Improved arrangements for encouraging dialogue between parents, schools and LEAs should be reflected in a reduction in the number of appeals to the SEN Tribunal.

By 2002...

3

- A revised version of the SEN Code of Practice will be in place, preserving the principles and safeguards of the present Code, while simplifying procedures and keeping paperwork to a minimum.

- There will be renewed emphasis on provision under the school-based stages of the Code of Practice, with support from LEAs and greater assurance for parents of effective intervention, particularly at stage 3.

- The result of these improvements will be that the proportion of children who need a statement will be moving towards 2%.

- The great majority of SEN assessments will be completed within the statutory timetable.

By 2002...

4

- A growing number of mainstream schools will be willing and able to accept children with a range of special educational needs: as a consequence, an increasing proportion of those children with statements of SEN who would currently be placed in special schools will be educated in mainstream schools.

- National and local programmes will be in place to support increased inclusion.

- Special and mainstream schools will be working together alongside and in support of one another.

By 2002...

5

- Regional planning machinery for SEN will be in place across England, helping to co-ordinate provision for low-incidence disabilities, specialist teacher training and other aspects of SEN.

- There will be clear guidance to support the effective development of special schools in the context of a policy of increased inclusion.

- New arrangements will be in place to safeguard the interests of children with special educational needs who are placed in independent schools.

By 2002...

6

- There will be a clear structure for teachers' professional development in SEN, from a strengthened attention to SEN issues in initial training through to improved training for headteachers, SEN co-ordinators and other SEN specialists.

- There will be a national framework for training learning support assistants.

- There will be national guidance on training governors to carry out their responsibilities for pupils with SEN.

- There will be national agreement on ways of reducing the time spent by educational psychologists on statutory assessments and maximising their contribution in the classroom, and the training necessary for their developing role.

By 2002...

7

- There will be new arrangements for disseminating up-to-date information about good practice in SEN provision.

- There will be improved co-operation and co-ordination between local education authorities, social services departments and health authorities, with the focus on meeting children's special needs more effectively.

- Speech and language therapy will be provided more effectively for children who need it.

- The Department will be collecting information about the experiences, once they have left school, of young people with SEN, to help schools and colleges prepare young people for adult life more effectively.

By 2002...

8

- A national programme will be in place to help primary schools tackle emotional and behavioural difficulties (EBD) at a very early stage.

- There will be enhanced opportunities for all staff to improve their skills in teaching children with emotional and behavioural difficulties.

- There will be a national programme to offer support to EBD special schools experiencing problems.

- There will be expanded support for schemes designed to renew the motivation of young people with emotional and behavioural difficulties at Key Stage 4.

1 *Policies for excellence*

Our policies for raising standards are for *all* children, including those with special educational needs (SEN). Early identification of difficulties and appropriate intervention will give children with SEN the best possible start to their school lives. Our initiatives for improving literacy and numeracy, introducing target setting for schools and opening up new technologies will help children with SEN reach their full potential.

What are special educational needs?

1   The term "special educational needs" can be misleading and lead to unhelpful assumptions. It may suggest that children with SEN are a readily-defined group, with common characteristics. It is sometimes used as though it applied only to the 3% of pupils with a statement of SEN. It is sometimes used of children from disadvantaged families. All this is far from the truth.

2   The law says that a child has special educational needs if he or she has:

- a learning difficulty (i.e. a significantly greater difficulty in learning than the majority of children of the same age, or a disability which makes it difficult to use the educational facilities generally provided locally); and if that learning difficulty calls for

- special educational provision (i.e. provision additional to, or different from, that made generally for children of the same age in local schools).

Whether or not a child has SEN will therefore depend both on the individual and on local circumstances. It may be entirely consistent with the law for a child to be said to have special educational needs in one school, but not in another.

3   In January 1997, schools said that 18% of their pupils – 1.5 million children – had special educational needs. Interpreting these figures is not straightforward. But, at the very least, many in this group will later be among the one-twelfth of young people who currently leave school without any GCSEs; and the one-sixth of adults with inadequate basic skills.

4   Success in our policies set out in *Excellence in schools*, particularly those aiming to tackle difficulties of literacy and numeracy at an early age, should enable schools to reduce over time the proportion of children they identify as having SEN. It would not be appropriate to set a target for this reduction. But we believe that, as our policies take effect, the proportion of secondary age children whom schools need to identify as having SEN should move closer to 10%. ***We will ensure that <u>all</u> our policies and programmes for schools are explicit about their implications for children with special educational needs.***

Early identification and early intervention

Very young children

5   The best way to tackle educational disadvantage is to get in early. When educational failure becomes entrenched, pupils can move from

demoralisation to disruptive behaviour and truancy. But early diagnosis and appropriate intervention improve the prospects of children with special educational needs, and reduce the need for expensive intervention later on. For some children, giving more effective attention to early signs of difficulties can prevent the development of SEN.

6   The majority of children with the most severe disabilities will be identified well before they start school; but health and social services professionals should also look for other factors which may lead to educational disadvantage. District Health Authorities and NHS Trusts are under a duty to bring to the LEA's attention any child under five who they think has SEN. An integrated approach by child health professionals, social services and education staff is needed right from the start, making full use of the children's services planning process.

7   To widen the options available, we want to encourage innovative partnerships between statutory and voluntary agencies. ***Multi-agency support for children with SEN will be a priority in our new pilot programme for early excellence centres.***

Case study

Multi-agency support for young children with SEN

STAR (St. Helens Advice and Resource) Children's Centre provides support for children with special needs and their families, from birth until the child starts school.

The Centre's steering group is made up of parents, representatives from the LEA, local NHS Trusts, social services and voluntary organisations. The staff team includes teachers, specialists in hearing and visual impairment, medical staff, therapists, an educational psychologist, a Portage and outreach support service, a nursery nurse and a social worker.

Parental involvement is an essential element of STAR's many activities, which include:

•   an assessment nursery

- a 'Starlight' parent and toddler group
- a Star communication group (supported by the local branch of the Association for all Speech Impaired Children – AFASIC)

- STARBEAM (Behaviour Education and Management) group

- STARDUST – a group for children with Down's Syndrome and their parents.

Local hospitals provide information about the Centre to all families of children born with disabilities. As children's special needs emerge, the Centre provides assessment and support. A developmental assessment of each child is made, and if necessary the child is referred to the LEA for statutory assessment. Each child takes a Record of Achievement on to school.

Pre-school education

8   In each LEA area, an early years development partnership will be established. Each will be fully representative of providers of early years services, including those with expertise in SEN, and will take into account the views of parents. Each partnership will draw up an Early Years Development Plan, which must show that appropriate provision will be available for children with SEN and that all providers, with support where necessary, are able to identify and assess special educational needs.

9   The new emphasis we are placing on early identification will mean that many children's special educational needs are identified before they reach compulsory school age. However, some children may slip through the net; others' special needs may not emerge until after they have started school.

Baseline assessment

10   From September 1998, all children will be assessed as they begin their primary education. Baseline assessment will not on its own establish whether individual pupils have special educational needs. But it will be crucial in helping to show where a child has problems which need attention – whether these arise from special needs, or from family or emotional difficulties. It should show teachers those pupils who need

a targeted teaching strategy or further classroom based assessment, perhaps leading to specific support from the school or from other agencies.

Literacy and numeracy

11   Literacy and numeracy are central building blocks for educational progress. The longer a child's basic skill deficiencies are left unaddressed, the less likely the child is to succeed at school or in later life. As a result, many children eventually receive statements of SEN and expensive additional provision. 40% of appeals to the SEN Tribunal concern literacy and numeracy difficulties of one sort or another.

12   We have set the target that 80% of all 11-year-olds should reach the standards expected for their age in English by the year 2002, with a corresponding figure of 75% for maths. We expect many children with SEN to reach these targets. These are ambitious targets, and we are putting in place initiatives to help pupils reach them. These include:

- reduced class sizes for our youngest pupils;

- introduction of a literacy hour in primary schools from September 1998; and

- introduction of a new National Curriculum for initial teacher training with greater focus on literacy and numeracy at primary level.

13   The Literacy Task Force has recommended:

- specific references to literacy in the SEN Code of Practice and in the individual education plans of children with SEN;

- attention to the implications of the national literacy target for children with special needs in programmes of professional development; and

- developing strategies to enable parents and schools to work together in supporting the literacy achievements of children with SEN.

We will build on these recommendations, and on those of the Numeracy Task Force, in our action programme for SEN.

14   As teachers become increasingly adept at tackling reading difficulties, children with specific learning difficulties (such as dyslexia) should in all but exceptional circumstances be catered for in mainstream schools without a statement. What is more, class-based strategies which help

children with specific learning difficulties can help children with literacy difficulties caused by other factors.

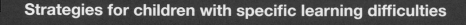

Case study

Strategies for children with specific learning difficulties

The DfEE is funding two research projects, based at the Helen Arkell Dyslexia Centre and Manchester Metropolitan University (MMU). These aim to assist teachers without specialist training to identify and help children with dyslexia in the course of their normal teaching. In both projects there are positive early findings about the effectiveness of some teaching strategies for all pupils, not just those with dyslexia.

There already exist a number of packages, some IT-based, which can help teachers and learning support assistants assess and help pupils with dyslexia.

15 The National Year of Reading in 1998/99 will focus on literacy skills: we need to make sure that children struggling with reading – for whatever reason – are encouraged to see themselves as improving readers. Consultations about the programme of events for the year will involve those with expertise in special educational needs.

QUESTION: How can we identify children's special educational needs earlier, and ensure that appropriate intervention addresses those needs?

School improvement and target setting

School improvement

16 *Excellence in schools* set out our proposals for school improvement. LEAs will prepare Education Development Plans (EDPs) showing how they will raise standards in their schools. A group of advisers from the Department's Standards and Effectiveness Unit, working with LEAs, will consider what SEN information should be included in EDPs.

17 Inspection of LEAs by OFSTED, assisted by the Audit Commission, will start in January 1998. These inspections will look at whether LEAs are fulfilling their statutory duties in relation to SEN and the standard of provision made for children with SEN. OFSTED is also improving its

procedures for inspecting schools, to increase the consistency and quality of inspection. There will be improved arrangements for vetting teams to inspect special schools, as well as a programme of professional development for inspectors. OFSTED will need to reflect the principles of this Green Paper in any revision of the Framework for the Inspection of Schools.

18   We want to establish the right climate in schools for all children to make the best possible progress. In some areas, years of social and economic deprivation have led to a culture of low expectation. Children from these communities may start at a disadvantage, but they are entitled to high expectations. We are consulting on the establishment of Education Action Zones to raise standards in areas with the highest levels of deprivation and under-achievement.

19   We want equally to challenge low expectations of children with SEN, a relatively high proportion of whom are boys. Some may be capable of achieving high standards across the board; others will show achievement in particular areas. Schools should build on pupils' strengths as well as addressing their needs.

20   Unfortunately, some schools fail to provide the quality of teaching and learning children need if expectations and achievement are to be raised. Of the mainstream schools so far inspected by OFSTED, 2% have been identified as failing. The corresponding figure for special schools is 7%, reflecting a particularly high rate of failure of schools for children with emotional and behavioural difficulties. We are concerned about this, and have put in hand a range of measures to ensure the rapid improvement of failing special schools (and of LEA pupil referral units). Our approach will combine pressure and support. Already a number of special schools have been restored to full health, sometimes through the "fresh start" outlined in *Excellence in schools*. But where a failing special school makes inadequate progress and seems unlikely to improve quickly, we will not hesitate to intervene and, if necessary, direct the LEA to close it.

Target setting

21   From September 1998 all schools, including special schools, will have to set challenging targets for pupil performance. Target setting will help schools and LEAs to focus effort and resources where they will have the greatest impact on raising standards, including the provision made for children with special educational needs.

Case study

Target setting at Marshfields Special School, Peterborough

Marshfields is a special school for pupils aged 5-18 with moderate learning difficulties. Many pupils also have sensory, physical, communication, emotional and/or behavioural difficulties. For the last few years the school has been developing the use of target setting in both educational and social areas of its work. Some examples of the targets Marshfields has set and how far these have been met include:

Target: All students to read at least 33% of 100 identified high frequency words at the end of Key Stage 3 and 50% at the end of Key Stage 4.
Evaluation: At the end of Key Stage 3, 72% of all students achieved the target set and at the end of Key Stage 4, 79% of all students did.

Target: Every primary phase student will learn to swim at least 5 metres.
Evaluation: By the end of the academic year, 37 out of 46 pupils (81%) achieved this target and over half of all students gained their 25 metres certificate.

Target: All middle phase students will use a cursive handwriting style.
Evaluation: By the end of the academic year every middle phase student had <u>attempted</u> a simple cursive handwriting style. 98% of pupils achieved the target but a small minority had insufficient fine motor skills to do so at this time.

22   For many schools, including special schools, target setting will present new challenges. As well as targets for academic performance, schools may need to set other targets which are relevant to children with SEN. These may, for example, relate to:

- pupils' behaviour, personal, social or life skills;

- numbers of pupils moving on to further education and training; or

- for some special schools, numbers of children who are successfully re-integrated into mainstream schools.

23 ***We will help mainstream and special schools to set realistic but challenging targets that are relevant to pupils with SEN, and to compare performance with other schools.*** Some LEAs are pioneering work in this area, and the Department's Standards and Effectiveness Unit will identify and disseminate this more widely. The DfEE will also fund research on target setting in special schools. OFSTED will make available to inspectors and schools aggregate data for special schools which will contribute to benchmarking and target setting.

QUESTION: What should the DfEE do to encourage and disseminate good practice in target setting for pupils with special educational needs, in both mainstream and special schools?

National Curriculum, assessment and qualifications

National Curriculum

24 The National Curriculum means that all pupils, including those with special educational needs, benefit from a broad and balanced curriculum. Pupils with SEN should have the same opportunities as others to progress and demonstrate achievement. At the same time, the National Curriculum should apply to these children in a way which teachers and parents recognise as appropriate. Access statements give teachers flexibility to match the National Curriculum to an individual pupil's ability. Modification and disapplication of subjects and assessments should therefore be needed only in exceptional cases.

25 Many special schools have worked hard to provide the full National Curriculum to their pupils. These schools have successfully challenged low expectations and differentiated the curriculum to meet a wide range of needs. The Qualifications and Curriculum Authority (QCA) has issued guidance on using a variety of approaches, within the flexibility of access statements, to present the National Curriculum to pupils with profound and multiple difficulties. It is working on guidance for pupils with emotional and behavioural difficulties and pupils with multi-sensory impairments. Schools will be invited to comment on strategies for delivering the curriculum to children with SEN when we conduct our review of the National Curriculum in due course.

QUESTION: How can we identify and disseminate good practice in delivering the curriculum to children with special educational needs?

Assessment

26   Key Stage 1-3 assessments are accessible to most pupils with SEN and help schools to measure their progress and achievements. Pupils working at the lowest levels at Key Stages 2 and 3 will be assessed only by their teacher. The National Curriculum tests provide for a range of adaptations and modifications to ensure that as many children as possible have access to them. However, it remains difficult to recognise and report the progress of pupils whose attainment will be below level 2 throughout their education. This issue is being considered by the QCA through the National Curriculum monitoring arrangements.

Qualifications

27   Most pupils with special educational needs can achieve some form of accredited qualification, such as GNVQs or GCSEs. But some – especially those in some special schools – are not given the opportunity to prove themselves in public examinations. All special schools should ask themselves whether more of their pupils may be capable of working towards such qualifications, given the special arrangements that can be made for pupils with special educational needs.

28   For pupils for whom GNVQs or GCSEs at sixteen are not appropriate, a range of nationally recognised qualifications – Certificates of Achievement – are available in all National Curriculum subjects and religious education. From September 1998, Certificates of Achievement will become part of the new Entry Level within the national framework of qualifications which will:

- allow full recognition of pupils' achievements;

- be recognised by colleges, employers and others in a way that some non-GCSE qualifications currently available are not;

- give more able pupils with SEN the opportunity to progress to higher level qualifications within the national framework; and

- give special schools key performance data for use in target setting and self-assessment.

29   Many teachers help pupils to identify and record their achievements and skills, often using the National Record of Achievement (NRA). The NRA is being replaced by the Progress File achievement planner, currently being

piloted in schools, including special schools. As part of Progress File, we will develop support material so that all pupils, including those with SEN, can identify and record their achievements, set goals and targets and plan their further learning.

QUESTION: Do the existing arrangements for assessment within the National Curriculum, and for public examinations, give appropriate recognition of the achievements of children with special educational needs? If not, how might they be improved?

The impact of Information and Communications Technology (ICT)

30 Developments in Information and Communications Technology are opening up educational opportunities previously denied to pupils with SEN. For example, speech recognition systems which operate word processing packages are becoming increasingly sophisticated. Speech Output and Large Print Systems are transforming the possibilities for visually impaired children to access the full range of curriculum materials. Some LEAs routinely assess ICT requirements of children with special educational needs. We want to see this good practice extended. ICT should be used to give children with special educational needs maximum access to the curriculum, and to help them reach their learning potential

31 Some ideas for using ICT to help children with special needs have been simple, and relatively cheap. The BT Fax Buddies project links children with communication difficulties to adult volunteers, including 12 from the DfEE's Special Educational Needs Division. The child and volunteer exchange one or two short faxes each week, to help the child become more accustomed to informal conversation. Fax machines are all that is required.

32 Expertise in ICT amongst professionals working with children with SEN varies. The National Grid For Learning will provide an infrastructure for networked learning, focusing initially on teacher development and curriculum support. *We will redeploy National Lottery funding towards the support of more specialised forms of ICT training for staff, including training in the use of ICT for children with SEN.* The new "Virtual Teachers' Centre" to be associated with the University for Industry will be an ideal forum for teachers to exchange ideas and good practice about special educational needs, extending the range of existing networks such as the SEN co-ordinators' discussion forum established by NCET.

Case study

Use of ICT to support children with SEN

West Oaks Special School in Leeds provides for children of all ages with a range of special educational needs, including autism. The school has made good use of IT, including use of networked specialist hardware and software to give children with communication and physical difficulties access to the curriculum.

The school has also worked for the National Council for Educational Technology (NCET) on its 'Superhighways' project; this led to a rapid development of skills among pupils and teachers and better access to all National Curriculum areas. The school's OFSTED report said that the recent development of effective IT teaching was due to *very positive leadership and substantial in-service training*. The report also said that some teachers were *demonstrating very good teaching... often planning activities designed to develop and reinforce basic communication skills and for older, more able pupils, providing IT skills to enhance their work in other subjects of the curriculum.*

QUESTION: What should the DfEE do to promote Information and Communications Technology as a means of supporting children with special educational needs?

SUMMARY

By 2002...

- The policies set out in *Excellence in schools* for raising standards, particularly in the early years, will be beginning to reduce the number of children who need long-term special educational provision.

- There will be stronger and more consistent arrangements in place across the country for the early identification of SEN.

- Schools and parents will have higher expectations of the standards children with SEN can attain.

- Target setting, in both mainstream and special schools, will take explicit account of the scope for improving the achievements of children with special educational needs.

- New Entry Level awards will be available for pupils for whom GNVQs or GCSEs at 16 are not appropriate.

- There will be more effective and widespread use of Information and Communications Technology to support the education of children with SEN, in both mainstream and special schools.

2 *Working with parents*

Parents of children with special educational needs face exceptional pressures. We want to help them cope with those pressures, and to give them real opportunities to influence and contribute to their child's education, working in partnership with schools, LEAs and other statutory and voluntary agencies.

Parents and families

1   *Excellence in schools* explained the importance we attach to parents' role in helping children learn. This role is nowhere more crucial than for the parents of children with special educational needs.

2   For many parents, learning of their child's problems will be a devastating blow. Nothing can entirely remove the pressures they will face, but much can be done to share them. There is no reason why any parent should feel the sense of not knowing where to turn which has been the experience of too many. In all our actions bearing on special educational needs, we shall take account of the effects on parents and families. We recognise that some parents will need support from a range of statutory and voluntary agencies if they are to help their children to flourish.

3   This is a strand running through this Green Paper. Its implications are discussed in more detail in some of the following chapters. Here we highlight three dimensions of parents' involvement:

*   choice;

*   entitlement;

*   partnership.

Choice

4   We want children with SEN to be educated in mainstream schools wherever possible. And we want to improve the way in which mainstream schools are able to meet special needs, so that most parents will want to choose a mainstream education for their child. But, as Chapter 4 explains, we will maintain parents' present right to express a preference for a special school place for their child, where they believe it necessary. And we shall ensure that, in opting for a mainstream school, parents of children with SEN have an increasing degree of real choice.

Entitlement

5   We want all parents of children with SEN to be confident that they know what the school will do to meet their child's needs. Chapter 3 explains that we want to improve the monitoring of school-based SEN provision, examining the case for a contract between school and parents for some children. As such measures improve parents' confidence in what the school

will deliver, and as schools become more confident in their own capabilities, we expect the present emphasis on statements of SEN to diminish. Indeed, we want it to do so: for some children at present, it is tying up resources in procedures, without producing real gains in support. But we unequivocally accept that the safeguards which are at present provided by statements – and in particular their guarantee of entitlement for children with complex special educational needs – must remain. All our measures will be designed to protect, or to enhance, the rights of vulnerable children and their parents.

Partnership

6   The knowledge parents have can help schools make the right provision for their child. Many schools and LEAs already spend much time working with parents. But sometimes this dialogue begins too late; sometimes it never gets started. When this happens, action to tackle a child's needs is delayed.

Supporting parents

7   Parents must be empowered to work with the school and local services to ensure that their child's needs are properly identified and met from the word go. The prospects of this are greatly improved where there is good practice such as:

- responding promptly to parents' questions, in face-to-face meetings wherever possible;

- actively seeking, and responding to, feedback from parents; and

- ensuring that, where necessary, parents are encouraged to make direct contact with the LEA officers dealing with their child's case.

8   Parents often value independent advice and support while their child is being assessed for a possible statement. The role of the "Named Person" could be important here. Under existing legislation, parents are offered this independent adviser only when a child receives a statement. *We believe that such an adviser should be available to all parents whose children's needs are being formally assessed.*

9   In recent years local SEN parent partnership schemes have helped LEAs to work more effectively with parents of children who are being assessed or have statements. Some schemes also offer support at earlier stages. But many schools are unfamiliar with local schemes. And the withdrawal of

financial support by the previous Government has put many schemes under pressure, bringing some to an end. From next year, parent partnership schemes will be eligible for support from the Standards Fund (which replaces GEST funding). ***We propose to encourage an expansion in the number and scope of parent partnership schemes.***

Case study

Parent partnership in Bradford

The parent partnership scheme in Bradford is based on three-way partnership between the LEA, Parent Link (a network of local parents and parent support groups) and Barnardo's. The responsibilities of each partner are clearly set out. The direction of the scheme is in the hands of a partnership committee, with parent representatives in the majority.

The scheme offers a resource and information base for parents and professionals working with children with SEN. Roadshows and seminars provide information to parents, and the scheme has recruited, trained and supported Named Persons. It has increased parents' involvement in their children's education, and helped to shape the LEA's policy and practice on SEN. As well as providing a service to families, the scheme maintains a developmental focus, currently working to help parents and teachers develop the skills necessary for effective dialogue.

The scheme works with many statutory and voluntary agencies, and makes an important contribution to Bradford's Children's Services Plan.

10 Parents are most likely to take an active part in school life and their child's development when they have clear information about the school's policies and their child's progress. But some parents with disabilities do not always gain access to the information which other parents can take for granted. We would be interested to hear from schools about how they have met the needs of disabled parents, and intend at a later stage to consult over guidance on accessible information.

11 Voluntary bodies and organisations of disabled people provide services which help parents learn about special educational needs, and offer advice and support for the whole family. Many work closely with parent partnership schemes and have contributed to the recruitment and training of Named Persons. We would like all local schemes to develop active links with voluntary bodies. *In line with the commitment in* **Excellence in schools** *to promote the effective use of family learning we shall offer financial support to continue and develop such work.*

QUESTION: **How can we make sure that parents receive the support they need at all stages of their child's education?**

Resolving disputes

12 Where children have complex needs, it is not always easy for parents and LEAs to reach agreement during the processes potentially leading to statutory assessment and statement. Approaches such as those described above should help. **We will consider whether to distil best practice into national guidelines.**

Case study

Parent Liaison Service, Somerset

Somerset's Parent Liaison Service was set up in January 1996. It offers an impartial mediation and conciliation service to parents who disagree with a school or the LEA.

The initial contact is often a parent's call to a helpline. The Parent Partnership Officer listens to the parent's problem, makes sure that the parent has all the relevant information and talks through possible action. This might involve the parent contacting the school or LEA, or the Parent Partnership Officer doing so on the parent's behalf. This often leads to a satisfactory outcome.

However, in about a quarter of cases, a meeting between the parent and LEA or school is arranged. The Parent Partnership Officer acts as a neutral third party. Areas of agreement and disagreement, and possible options, are explored. Agreement on some action is reached in about two-thirds of these cases. Where a case does have to proceed to the SEN Tribunal, the aim is that it should not do so simply because of a failure of communication. The number of appeals to the Tribunal from Somerset fell by 17% last year, compared with an increase nationally of 26%.

The Parent Liaison Service also runs workshops for Named Persons, SEN co-ordinators, other teachers and learning support assistants which include an element of basic conflict resolution and mediation.

13   In a small proportion of cases, something more may be needed. We shall consider whether to require LEAs to offer parents a conciliation meeting, where necessary, at key decision points. It would be important to make sure that any such arrangement did not further delay effective provision. If conciliation failed, parents would – unless they unreasonably refused to agree to a conciliation meeting – be able to proceed with an appeal to the independent SEN Tribunal.

QUESTION: **How can we encourage dialogue between parents, schools and LEAs, and resolve disputes about special educational needs as early as possible?**

The SEN Tribunal

14   The Tribunal is the final arbiter in disputes between parents and LEAs. Its overriding aim is to consider the needs of the child. Each appeal is heard by a panel of three – a legally trained chairman, and two members with expertise in SEN and/or local government.

	1994/95	1995/96	1996/97
Appeals Registered	1,092	1,551	1,969
Of these:			
• Appeals Withdrawn (no.)	482	752	**
• Appeals Withdrawn (%)	44	48	**
Average time taken for appeals (months)	5*	5.5*	4

* Average time includes English and Welsh cases
** Not yet available. The Tribunal currently predicts a similar rate of withdrawal for 1996/97 as for 1995/96.

Figure 1: Appeals before the SEN Tribunal (England)

15   The Tribunal is in general operating effectively. It is a good deal faster than the system of appeals to the Secretary of State it replaced. A number of specific suggestions for improving its effectiveness have however been made. For example, it has been suggested that, without being bound by them, the Tribunal should be required to take account of the LEA's policies on provision for children with SEN.

QUESTION: **Are changes needed to improve the effectiveness of the SEN Tribunal?**

SUMMARY

By 2002...

- All parents whose children are being assessed for a statement of SEN will be offered the support of an independent "Named Person".

- Parent partnership schemes will be in place in every LEA in England, and will play an important part in supporting parents of children with SEN.

- Improved arrangements for encouraging dialogue between parents, schools and LEAs should be reflected in a reduction in the number of appeals to the SEN Tribunal.

3 *Practical support: the framework for SEN provision*

A robust framework for assessing and monitoring special educational needs is essential. But too often at present resources intended to support children with SEN are being diverted to procedures and paperwork. We want to achieve high quality provision with less emphasis on the need for statements.

Code of Practice

1   The *Code of Practice on the Identification and Assessment of Special Educational Needs* gives statutory guidance to schools, LEAs, health authorities and social services departments. It sets out a five-stage framework for meeting children's special educational needs, involving parents at every stage. Stages 1-3 are school-based. In general, action at stages 1 and 2, including drawing up an Individual Education Plan (IEP) setting out targets for the child, falls entirely to the school. At stage 3 the school will normally look for some outside support, from educational psychologists or LEA learning support staff. Stage 4 is a transitional stage where the LEA considers the need for, and if appropriate arranges, a multi-agency assessment of a child's SEN. The provision for the child will usually continue as at stage 3 during the assessment. At stage 5, the LEA considers the need for a statement of SEN and, if appropriate, draws up a statement and arranges, monitors and reviews provision for the child.

2   The Code has made a difference, and for the better. Its principles are widely supported. OFSTED reports reflect the progress schools have made. Parents have welcomed the opportunities it gives them to take an active part in their child's education. We do not want to change its basic principles or the broad thrust of the associated legislation.

3   But schools have expressed concern about the cost of implementing the guidance in the Code, and about the 'bureaucracy' resulting from it, particularly in relation to IEPs and annual reviews of statements. It has been suggested that, too often, attention is focused on getting the paperwork right, at the expense of providing practical support to the child. We want to correct this imbalance.

4   Subject to consultation on this Green Paper, *we propose to revise the Code to address these and other points.* In doing so we shall take account of the views of the new Working Group on Reducing Bureaucratic Burdens on Teachers. The process might begin in March 1998 with a consultation paper distributed widely for comment, leading in the autumn to consultation on a draft revised Code. On this timetable, the revised Code could be in place from September 1999.

5   Issues which we shall consider in any revision include:

- provision for the under-fives;

- bringing out the flexibility which schools have to interpret the Code's guidance in the light of their own circumstances;

- whether we need to redefine and perhaps combine some of the stages of the Code;

- how the guidance in the Code on IEPs and annual reviews of statements might be amended to reduce paperwork, and to build on other developments, such as baseline assessment;

- how to meet the different circumstances of primary, secondary and special schools; and

- whether the Code should say more about children whose first language is not English.

QUESTION: **Will it be helpful to review the Code of Practice, with a view to a revised version in 1999? If so, which aspects of the Code need particular attention? How can we reduce the paperwork associated with the Code?**

Improving provision at stages 1-3 of the Code of Practice

6   Parents need to be confident that effective help will be provided by schools at stages 1-3 of the Code of Practice. For many children, special educational needs will be transitory. Support at stages 1-3 for a year or two will be all that is needed. But the amount and quality of extra help given to children at these stages varies from school to school, both within and between LEAs. The point at which schools conclude that such support has been ineffective and ask the LEA to assess a child for a statement also varies widely.

7   Schools' ability to meet the needs of children with SEN will develop only if staff are able to draw on relevant expertise. We believe that LEAs should help schools improve the quality of provision for SEN by:

- monitoring the quality of provision at stages 1-3, and reporting their conclusions to headteachers and governors;

- helping schools to develop, implement and review their SEN policies; and providing more advice on aspects of SEN *practice* (as distinct from *documentation*);

- enabling educational psychologists and LEA learning support staff to spend more time working with children in schools and helping teachers improve their skills in meeting the needs of children at stages 1-3;

- supporting e-mail links between schools and SEN support services to give prompt help to SEN co-ordinators (SENCOs) and other teachers;

- encouraging schools to improve staff expertise through professional development or, for example, by arranging for local SENCOs to exchange ideas on good practice;

- collecting and comparing SEN data for mainstream schools, and disseminating benchmark and good practice information to schools.

Case study

SEN policies in Newham

Newham LEA has helped its schools develop their SEN policies and has demonstrated the value of an LEA-wide approach. All schools were asked to send a copy of their SEN policy to the LEA. The LEA's officers reviewed all the policies against the statutory requirements. Schools were subsequently given an individual report commenting on both the positive features of their policy and the areas needing attention. The LEA also gave schools guidance on issues highlighted by the policies submitted. Newham schools have developed and updated their policies in the light of this advice.

QUESTION: **How can LEAs help schools improve the quality of provision at stages 1-3 of the Code of Practice?**

8   Improvements in the quality of provision at stages 1-3 should reduce the need for some children to move to a statutory assessment. Parents will however want to be certain that the school is doing all it can to help their child at stage 3, with support where necessary from outside services. There is a case for strengthening the assurance on this. One option would be for schools to offer a contract to parents at stage 3 – essentially, a strengthened IEP – specifying the agreed special educational provision the child would receive from inside and outside the school and the support which the parents would be expected to give.

9   The aim for most children with SEN should be to move back down the stages of the Code of Practice once intervention has successfully begun to address the child's difficulties. In this way, support will become increasingly school-based and class-based. But as structured help is gradually withdrawn, schools will often need to continue with flexible approaches – whether in terms of time or access to special facilities – so that the child does not suffer from too sudden a transition.

QUESTION: **How can we strengthen the assurance to parents that schools will offer effective and consistent support at stages 1- 3 of the Code of Practice? Should we introduce contracts between schools and parents specifying the agreed extra provision the child will receive at stage 3?**

Statements

10   For children with complex needs, statements fulfil three main functions. They are used:

- to define a child's needs;

- to specify provision to meet those needs; and

- to co-ordinate this provision by saying who will do what.

11   For several reasons, the statement has often come to be seen as central to SEN provision. When the Code was introduced, it was envisaged that the needs of the great majority of children with SEN should be met effectively under its school-based stages, and that only in a minority of cases, perhaps the 2% of children envisaged by the Warnock Report in 1978, would the LEA need to carry out a statutory assessment of SEN and make a statement. But there has been a steep increase in recent years, so that 233,000 pupils (almost 3%) now have statements.

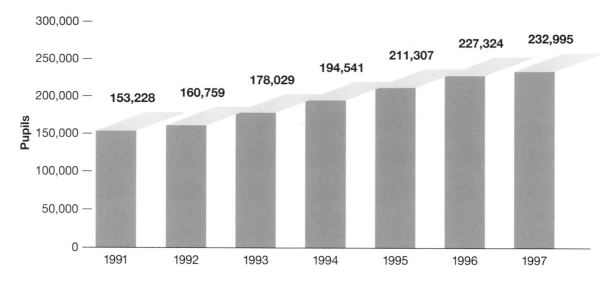

Figure 2: The number of pupils with statements 1991 – 1997

The growth has been most marked in mainstream primary and secondary schools, where numbers of pupils with statements more than doubled from 62,000 in January 1991 to 134,000 in January 1997.

12 The recent rapid increase in the number of statements has unwelcome effects:

- the process for assessing pupils and issuing statements is lengthy and expensive, and increased numbers put greater pressure on it;

- resources that could be used to give practical support to pupils are being diverted into procedures;

- resources allocated to those with statements are diverted away from the majority of children with SEN but without statements;

- statements can act as barriers to full inclusion of pupils with SEN. They can limit schools' flexibility; where mainstream classes include several pupils with statements, the combined effect of the individual statements each specifying particular special educational provision can hinder effective use of support across the whole class.

13 The legal framework and funding practice combine to emphasise the difference between having and not having a statement, and add to the pressure on parents and schools to seek a statutory assessment. At the same time LEAs, acutely conscious of sharply rising SEN budgets and, in some cases, seeking to provide stronger support in the earlier stages of the Code of Practice, have sought ways of restricting the rise in the

number of statements. There is potential for mistrust and conflict in an area where trust and co-operation are essential.

14 We acknowledge the necessary role currently played by multi-agency assessments and statements in ensuring that the needs of children with the most significant and complex SEN are fully considered, and appropriate provision determined. At present we do not intend to amend the central place of statements in law. But we believe that current practice gives them excessive prominence. We are committed to the principle that the needs of the great majority of children who have SEN should be met effectively by mainstream schools, with support where necessary but without the need for statutory intervention by LEAs.

15 Moreover, we want to look at the way statements work for those children who need them. In the light of the response to this Green Paper, we will consider:

- whether we should define national criteria for statements or set out expectations for numbers of statements (see paragraphs 16-19);

- whether the content of statements is appropriate (see paragraphs 20-21);

- how to ensure that annual reviews of statements are used for a fundamental examination of the child's progress (see paragraph 22);

- how to ensure that the new framework for funding under local management of schools (LMS) supports the developments we seek (see Appendix 2); and

- how to ensure that statutory assessments are completed within the set timescales (see paragraph 23).

In the longer term we will consider whether statements in their present form are the best way of carrying out the functions described in paragraph 10 above, or whether – while maintaining existing safeguards – these might be better achieved by some alternative means.

National criteria

16 There are wide variations between LEAs in making statements. In some LEA areas fewer than 2% of pupils have statements; in others the proportion exceeds 4%. The reasons for such variation include underlying differences in the socio-economic make-up of different areas, and the extent to which LEAs specifically delegate funding for SEN so that schools can provide for children without the need for statements. In some parts of the country there is substantial movement of children with statements between LEAs. But these factors do not explain the full extent of the variation.

Metropolitan Districts

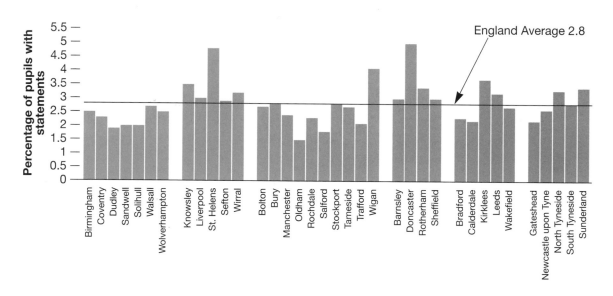

New Unitary Authorities and Non-Metropolitan Counties

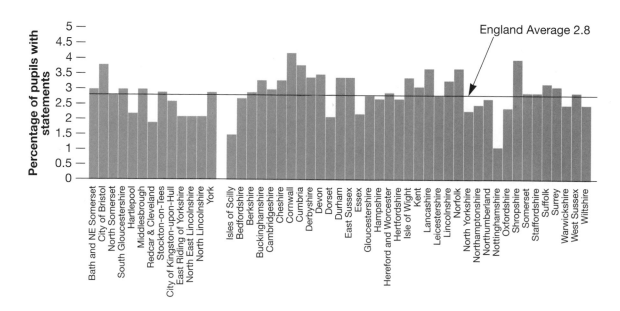

Inner and Outer London

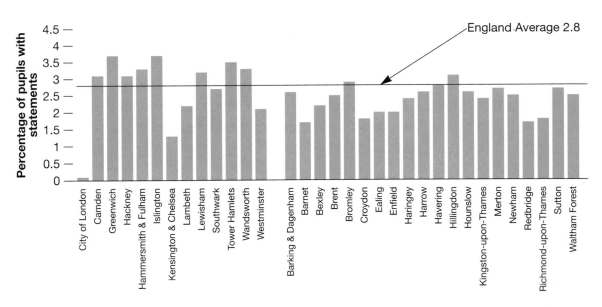

Figure 3: Variation in percentages of pupils with statements in LEA areas, January 1997

17   There are similar variations between schools' practices in placing children on their SEN registers or at particular stages of the Code. In January 1997, 4% of primary and secondary schools in England (800 schools) assessed 40% or more of their pupils as having SEN whilst 9% (1900) identified fewer than 5% of their pupils as having SEN.

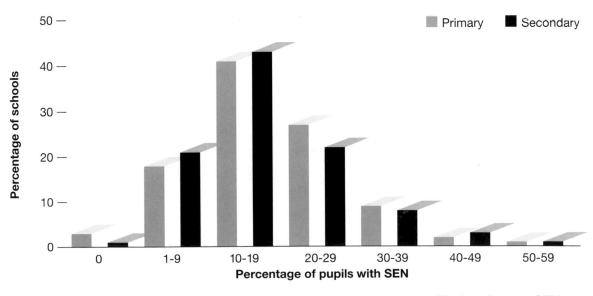

Figure 4: Variations between schools in proportion of children identified as having SEN, January 1997

18 The view is sometimes expressed that these variations would be reduced if there were national criteria for statements or for each stage of the Code of Practice. We are not convinced that this is so. LEAs' local criteria for statements are often very similar, but do not seem to lead to uniformity of decision making. It is not self-evident that the introduction of national criteria would have any greater impact. However, we do not discount the arguments in favour of more national consistency, and would welcome views. One possibility would be to publish a non-statutory guide, drawing on the existing criteria used by LEAs.

National expectations for numbers of statements

19 We could, alternatively, set a national expectation of the proportion of children who might benefit from statements, and perhaps of the proportions of pupils to be expected nationally at stages of the Code of Practice. These could not override the duty to meet individual children's needs. They would therefore not operate as strict quotas: there could be legitimate reasons why LEAs – and certainly why individual schools – should deviate from them. But, on this model, we would expect LEAs and schools, as well as those involved in resolving disagreements, to have regard to them in setting their criteria for assessing needs. For example, we might adopt a national average expectation that say 2% of children would have statements, with an expected range between individual LEAs from say 1.5% to 2.5% according to factors such as their socio-economic characteristics and local approaches at stage 3. We might expect LEAs to set out – perhaps in their Education Development Plans – what they would do to take such expectations into account.

QUESTION: **How might we secure greater national consistency in making statements, or in supporting children at the other stages of the Code of Practice?**

Content of statements

20 A statement must set out both a child's educational and non-educational needs and the provision to be made in each case. The distinction between the two is often unclear. Speech therapy, psychological support or provision of specialised equipment, for example, can benefit a child's educational progress even if provided for health reasons. We favour dropping this distinction. But we recognise that this would require changes to LEAs' statutory responsibility for implementing statements, or to the arrangements for funding provision under a statement. Possible changes in funding of therapy services are discussed in Chapter 7.

21 Where children are placed in a special school or unit, there may be other questions we need to ask about the content of statements. For example:

- can the statement acknowledge that specialist environment by being less detailed in some respects than a statement for a mainstream placement?

- should the statement set out the progress that would be needed for the child to move to a mainstream setting?

Reviewing statements

22 We believe that, when a statement is reviewed, greater consideration should be given to whether it continues to be appropriate for the child. A pupil should not necessarily need a statement for his or her whole school career. But, currently, very few statements are discontinued; of those in force in January 1996, fewer than 3,000 – around 1% of the total – were discontinued in the following 12 months for children below statutory school leaving age. We propose that statements should include a greater emphasis on expected educational outcomes, and that in appropriate cases they should say that they would end on the achievement of specified outcomes. Too often, at present, parents and schools fear the cessation of a statement. We need to move to a situation where the achievement of the objectives in a statement is seen for the success it is, permitting the child to move to support at stage 3 of the Code: a stage 3 in which parents would have confidence following the changes proposed in this chapter.

QUESTION: **What changes should be made to the contents of, or monitoring and review arrangements for, statements of SEN?**

Time limits for producing statements

23 Alongside the other measures proposed in this chapter, we shall press LEAs to complete assessments within the set timescales. Some LEAs have excellent records. But Audit Commission figures for 1995-96 showed that only 40% of draft statements in England and Wales were prepared within the statutory eighteen week limit. Parents do not find this acceptable. We will expect to see substantial improvement so that pupils with the most significant SEN can have their needs met promptly. *We will investigate the causes of delay, identify good practice, promulgate it, and challenge those LEAs with poor performance to improve.*

SUMMARY

By 2002...

- A revised version of the SEN Code of Practice will be in place, preserving the principles and safeguards of the present Code, while simplifying procedures and keeping paperwork to a minimum.

- There will be renewed emphasis on provision under the school-based stages of the Code of Practice, with support from LEAs and greater assurance for parents of effective intervention, particularly at stage 3.

- The result of these improvements will be that the proportion of children who need a statement will be moving towards 2%.

- The great majority of SEN assessments will be completed within the statutory timetable.

4 *Increasing inclusion*

The ultimate purpose of SEN provision is to enable young people to flourish in adult life. There are therefore strong educational, as well as social and moral, grounds for educating children with SEN with their peers. We aim to increase the level and quality of inclusion within mainstream schools, while protecting and enhancing specialist provision for those who need it. We will redefine the role of special schools to bring out their contribution in working with mainstream schools to support greater inclusion.

The principle of inclusion

1   We want to see more pupils with SEN included within mainstream primary and secondary schools. We support the United Nations Educational, Scientific and Cultural Organisation (UNESCO) Salamanca World Statement on Special Needs Education 1994. This calls on governments to adopt the principle of inclusive education, enrolling all children in regular schools, unless there are compelling reasons for doing otherwise. That implies the progressive extension of the capacity of mainstream schools to provide for children with a wide range of needs.

2   The needs of individual children are paramount. Where these cannot currently be met in mainstream schools, specialist provision should be available. But it should not be assumed that all children requiring specialist provision at a particular time will do so permanently, nor that the current capacity of mainstream schools to respond to their needs cannot be extended. We want to develop an education system in which specialist provision is seen as an integral part of overall provision, aiming wherever possible to return children to the mainstream and to increase the skills and resources available in mainstream schools. We therefore want to strengthen links between special and mainstream schools, and to ensure that LEA support services are used to support mainstream placements.

3   Inclusion is a process, not a fixed state. By inclusion, we mean not only that pupils with SEN should wherever possible receive their education in a mainstream school, but also that they should join fully with their peers in the curriculum and life of the school. For example, we believe that – taking account of any normal arrangements for setting – children with SEN should generally take part in mainstream lessons rather than being isolated in separate units. But separate provision may be necessary on occasion for specific purposes, and inclusion must encompass teaching and curriculum appropriate to the child's needs. Many schools will need to review and adapt their approaches in order to achieve greater inclusion.

Case study

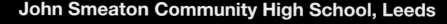

John Smeaton Community High School, Leeds

John Smeaton Community High School, Leeds, has adopted a policy of working towards inclusive education for all. The school's roll includes students with moderate or severe learning difficulties, visual and hearing impairments and physical difficulties.

The school's 1996 OFSTED report noted that the quality of teaching was a particular strength, with good planning and use of individualised teaching programmes to meet the needs of pupils with SEN. Such pupils were fully integrated into mainstream school life and lessons, and the personal development of all pupils was enhanced as a consequence of the diverse intake of the school.

4   We recognise that there is a variety of views on the sensitive issue of where individual children with SEN might best prosper. We recognise the concerns of some parents about whether and how the needs of their child will be met in a mainstream school. We also recognise that schools and LEAs are at different starting points in considering the issue of inclusion. Our approach will be practical, not dogmatic. Decisions about individual children must take account of all their circumstances, not least their educational experiences to date. Parents will continue to have the right to express a preference for a special school where they consider this appropriate to their child's needs.

Inclusion within mainstream schools

5   There is no reason why children with similar needs in different parts of the country should not have similar opportunities to attend mainstream schools. Yet at present there is wide variation in the percentage of children in each LEA who are educated in special schools, ranging from under 0.5% in some areas to over 2% in others. Across the country as a whole, some 98,000 pupils are educated in maintained or non-maintained special schools, a number which has been virtually constant throughout the 1990s.

6   Different factors bear on the scope for inclusion for those with different types of SEN. For some with physical disabilities, improved access to and within school buildings may be the fundamental first step. New technology can help improve access to the curriculum and limit pupils' communication difficulties. Many pupils with mild or moderate learning difficulties or sensory impairments and some with severe and complex needs are, with appropriate learning support, already thriving in mainstream school settings, and enriching the whole school community.

Case study

Inclusion in Manchester

Manchester LEA believes that, where appropriate, children with physical difficulties and severe learning difficulties should be educated in mainstream schools. Under Manchester's Barrier Free Partnership two secondary schools and a network of feeder primary schools have received capital support to help them become completely accessible to pupils with physical disabilities. Schools' own efforts are supplemented by support teams (teachers and learning assistants) who help individual pupils or groups with physical difficulties and severe learning difficulties.

Newall Green High School is one of the schools benefiting from Manchester's inclusion policy. It offers additionally resourced provision for children with physical difficulties and severe learning difficulties in the south of the city. The school has been barrier free since September last year. Ramps, lifts and new equipment, such as height adjustable work areas, have been installed. The support team has helped pupils gain access to the curriculum, and is working with the children so that, in due course, they will be able to carry on without support. The school's recent OFSTED report noted that all pupils with SEN are fully integrated into the life and work of the school.

7   There are many practical steps which we could take to promote greater inclusion in mainstream schools for pupils with SEN. We could:

- require LEAs to <u>prepare and submit plans for taking inclusion forward</u>, perhaps within the framework of their Education Development Plans;

- suggest that in the first instance priority should be given to securing inclusion for younger children or those with particular forms of SEN, perhaps those with physical disabilities, sensory impairments or with moderate learning difficulties. We could change the law so that <u>LEAs would have to secure a mainstream school placement for such pupils where this accorded with their parents' wishes.</u> This would not mean that parents would have unconstrained choice. But it would mean that the LEA had to ensure that an accessible mainstream school was available;

- require all children to be registered on the roll of a mainstream school, supported as appropriate by specialist provision (which for some children might mean placement in a special school, at least for part of their school career);

- direct increased levels of capital support to extend the existing Schools Access Initiative. Support totalling £4 million a year is currently available for schemes to improve physical access to mainstream schools and access to the curriculum within such schools. We plan to increase significantly the scale of this Initiative from 1998;

- target specific grant towards measures which would enhance mainstream schools' ability to include pupils with SEN. Grants could be earmarked for disability awareness training and SEN-specific training of teachers and others in mainstream schools. Or we could provide pump-priming support to LEAs which commit themselves to greater levels of inclusion, to assist with transitional costs of running both mainstream and special school provision;

- seek ways of celebrating the success of those schools which improve their ability to provide for a wide range of special needs. For example, we could set standards for schools in improving their ability to provide for a wide range of special needs and encourage all schools to achieve these. We could develop a "kite mark" for schools which reached the standards;

- give some priority for capital support where possible to planned school reorganisations which would enhance SEN provision in mainstream schools, or facilitate the co-location of special and mainstream schools, in preference to reorganisations which would increase separate special school places.

In parallel with such action, a new Ministerial Task Force will review existing legislation in order to implement our manifesto commitment to people with disabilities. This will include the treatment of education within the Disability Discrimination Act.

8   We do not underestimate the difficulties of any of this. We are asking a lot of schools, and not only in relation to SEN, over the next few years. Some parents may fear their children will lose out if teachers focus their attention

on pupils with SEN. We acknowledge the need to develop an ethos of positive approaches to children with disabilities. We need to find ways of helping LEAs to shift resources from separate provision towards support for inclusion. As resources become available, it will be necessary to identify priorities for action. In some cases, pilot schemes may be the way forward. In the meantime we shall work with LEAs and schools with relevant experience, to consider the necessary conditions for promoting inclusion more widely. We shall also fund research to assess the relative costs, benefits and practical implications of educating children in mainstream and special schools. Increasing levels of inclusion for SEN pupils will be a continuing process; as technology, skills and confidence develop, so will the scope for inclusion.

QUESTION: What priority measures should we take to include more pupils with special educational needs within mainstream schools?

Admission arrangements for children with SEN

9   The White Paper *Excellence in schools* signalled important reforms in the way school admission arrangements are to be agreed and co-ordinated. Local forums of headteachers and governors will be encouraged to discuss admission arrangements in their areas, and any disagreements between admission authorities which cannot be resolved through dialogue will in most cases be settled by an independent adjudicator. A new statutory Code of Practice will be binding on all admission authorities, and on the adjudicator.

10   These new arrangements will have important implications for the admission of children with SEN but without statements. The admissions Code of Practice will stress that such children must be treated no less favourably than other applicants. The new voluntary forums will be able to take stock of the overall impact and operation of local arrangements on the admission of pupils with SEN, and the adjudicator will if necessary resolve disagreements. For children with statements the arrangements confirming access to the school named in the statement will continue.

11   It is sometimes suggested that schools may be reluctant to admit pupils with SEN because of their possible impact on a school's standing in the performance tables. From 1998, the transition to locally published primary school tables will give LEAs the flexibility to include more data and background information to set results in context. Value added measures in both primary and secondary tables will mean that success in raising the levels of achievement of children with SEN receives fuller recognition.

QUESTION: What should the proposed Code of Practice on admissions say about the admission of pupils with SEN?

A new role for special schools

12   Traditionally, the role of special schools has been to provide specialist teaching, support and facilities to meet the needs of pupils who attend their school. This has meant a concentration of experience and expertise in a small number of schools (about 5% of the total) meeting the needs of 1% of pupils. We recognise the continuing need for special schools to provide – in some cases temporarily – for a very small proportion of pupils whose needs cannot be fully met within the mainstream sector. The context in which they operate has however changed over the past decade. The categorisation of special schools is no longer as clear as it might once have been, and many now cater for a wide range of increasingly complex needs.

13   If we are to move successfully to greater inclusion, it is essential that pupils with complex SEN in mainstream schools receive specialist support. The role of special schools should reflect this changing context. In principle, teachers in special schools are uniquely equipped to help their colleagues in mainstream schools to meet complex needs. But currently there are no requirements for special and mainstream schools to co-operate. Arrangements do exist, but their incidence is patchy and there is little co-ordination. *We will examine how special school staff can work more closely with mainstream schools and support services to meet the needs of all pupils with SEN.*

Case study

Round Oak School and Support Service, Warwickshire

Round Oak was opened in 1989 following the closure of two special schools. It provides flexibility for children with moderate learning difficulties through its core special school and eight linked cluster mainstream schools. Pupils are educated in a variety of settings, from total inclusion in mainstream classes through to separate provision when necessary. Liaison between core and cluster staff means that children can move between settings as their needs change.

Many of the children that Round Oak supports are enrolled

at a cluster school, and spend their entire school week at their mainstream school. OFSTED recently reported that the progress of pupils in the cluster schools is "always at least satisfactory and frequently good. They are able to keep pace in their mainstream setting and enjoy positive support from cluster staff".

Round Oak has many distinctive features:

- all staff are appointed to the core school but can move flexibly throughout the system – eight teaching and some part-time non-teaching staff are currently deployed to the cluster schools to support children with statements;

- special school pupils have access to subject specialists at all four Key Stages; and

- the cluster schools provide SEN support to a number of other primary and secondary schools.

14   If we are to broaden the contributions made by special schools and their staff, the small size of many special schools (the majority have fewer than 80 pupils) may make some desirable developments difficult. LEAs will need to consider whether in some cases:

- staff currently working in special schools might work in resourced mainstream schools, or in units attached to mainstream schools; or

- some special schools might be amalgamated – wherever possible in close association with mainstream schools – to create larger special schools whose teachers would have an explicit remit to provide support and training to mainstream colleagues and to individual children.

15   We want to build on existing good practice. Possible ways forward are:

- guidance to LEAs and schools on co-operative working. This might cover:

  - shared facilities;

  - shared teaching and non-teaching expertise;

  - support for pupils who move between special and mainstream schools;

- special schools becoming part of cluster arrangements with primary and secondary schools;

- suggesting that LEAs include in their Education Development Plans (EDPs) arrangements for collaboration within the framework of generally inclusive provision, including targets for improvement. LEA plans would reflect any arrangements agreed at regional level (see Chapter 5), and would be subject to inspection by OFSTED;

- extending LEAs' duty to review the provision they make for pupils with SEN, to include a requirement to review collaborative arrangements between schools;

- placing a requirement on special and mainstream schools to provide details of collaborative arrangements in their annual reports. For special schools, this could include setting targets for the amount of time pupils should participate in mainstream education.

The local forums on admissions mentioned above should encourage co-operation on the admission policies of mainstream and special schools.

16 In all this there are exciting opportunities for special schools. Increasingly, they will be providing a varied pattern of support for children with SEN. Some children will be in full time placements, others part-time or short-term; staff will be supporting some children in mainstream placements; they will be helping mainstream schools to implement inclusion policies; and they will be a source of training and advice for mainstream colleagues. It may be that when their role has developed to this extent, the term "special school" will be seen as an inadequate reflection of what they do.

17 This is a challenging agenda. Our proposals will have significant resource implications, not least in the training which some special school teachers will need as their role develops. *We shall start with pilot projects, drawing on the experience which some LEAs and schools are developing in this area.* But we want to see real progress over the next four years.

QUESTION: How can we help special schools to develop their role, working more closely with mainstream schools to meet the needs of all pupils with SEN?

SUMMARY

By 2002...

- A growing number of mainstream schools will be willing and able to accept children with a range of special educational needs: as a consequence, an increasing proportion of those children with statements of SEN who would currently be placed in special schools will be educated in mainstream schools.

- National and local programmes will be in place to support increased inclusion.

- Special and mainstream schools will be working together alongside and in support of one another.

5 *Planning SEN provision*

Whether in mainstream or special schools, children with the most severe and complex difficulties will continue to need specialist support. We shall encourage regional co-operation so that specialist facilities, whether from the maintained, voluntary or private sectors, are available when and where they are needed. LEAs will make decisions about changes to their special schools in the light of this regional co-operation and guidance from the Government.

Planning: the regional dimension

Role of local education authorities

1   LEAs are providers both of school places for pupils with special educational needs, and of specialist support services. However, as a result of this mainly <u>local</u> focus, we find across the country:

- differences in access to, and in quality of, provision; with duplication in some cases, and under-provision in others;

- wide variations in funding levels;

- inconsistency among schools in seeking external support; and

- difficulties for some smaller authorities in providing for pupils who need very specialised provision.

2   There can legitimately be variation in the ways in which educational services are provided, and to some extent in the degree of choice locally. But there can be no argument for variations in quality. *We will work to secure a continuum of provision across the country so that, no matter where pupils live and whatever their needs, an appropriate level of support is available.*

3   While it may be possible for the largest LEAs to make provision for a wide range of special needs, we do not believe that a go-it-alone approach will lead to resources being used efficiently and effectively. Nor will smaller authorities find it easy to provide the range of specialist services necessary to support the improvements we seek. In some areas, collaborative arrangements operate successfully, involving the voluntary and private sectors as well as other LEAs. But in general there is a need for closer co-operation.

Regional planning

4   For these reasons *we want to see the development of regional planning arrangements for some aspects of SEN provision.* Statutory responsibility for SEN would remain with the LEA. The regional arrangements would help LEAs meet that responsibility by opening up access to all available resources. We want social services departments and health authorities, and the voluntary and independent sectors, to be fully included as partners in the arrangements, so that their contribution can be properly integrated into the regional framework.

Case study

Cross-LEA provision in inner London

A consortium of five inner London LEAs, led by Islington, was set up, initially using Grants for Education Support and Training (GEST) funding, to make provision for pupils with multi-sensory impairments.

In partnership with Sense (The National Deafblind and Rubella Association), the LEAs contracted one of its teachers – a national expert on working with these pupils – to conduct an initial audit of need, and then to support an advisory teacher employed by the consortium. The advisory teacher initially spent one day a week in schools in each of the authorities working with pupils, teachers and other staff, advising on individual programmes for pupils and providing training. Latterly, she has linked with other agencies in education, health and social services and spent one week in each school providing more specific support.

5   We do not propose to develop statutory or excessively formal arrangements. Their success will depend on partnership. Our preferred option, therefore, is to encourage voluntary co-operation on a regional basis, between LEAs, and between LEAs and other statutory, voluntary and private sector providers, including non-maintained special schools and independent schools catering for SEN, and institutions providing teacher training. This co-operation would be reinforced through funding mechanisms.

6   The core functions of these arrangements might be:

-   planning of places for low incidence disabilities, such as visual and hearing impairments and at the profound end of the autistic spectrum;

-   encouraging co-operation and perhaps specialisation in SEN support services;

-   developing provision for specialised in-service teacher training;

-   collecting and comparing data on SEN provision.

These are not the only areas that might benefit from regional planning.

Others – for example, provision for pupils who are out of school because of illness or injury – might be included. Some voluntary organisations have begun to study the issues involved in bringing about such co-operation: we are supporting this work.

7 Regional planning arrangements could be facilitated in the first instance by Government Offices (GOs). The sort of arrangements we envisage are:

- groups to be made up of LEAs, other statutory agencies, voluntary and private sector representatives and providers of training, brought together on a voluntary basis under the chairmanship of the GO; membership could in some cases draw on existing regional structures; DfEE's SEN Division would attend meetings;

- the structure would be non-bureaucratic; the GO would provide "light touch" facilitation; LEA staff or others with SEN background would be seconded to the GO to provide support for the regional groups;

- each group would be expected to produce a regional plan for relevant aspects of SEN provision within the context of increasing inclusion; the DfEE could issue guidance on coverage;

- as a first step we might support pilot schemes based in two GOs to prepare for introduction of these arrangements;

- LEAs would be expected to contribute to the low-level administrative costs of the arrangements; regional planning should result in better value for money through more economical use of expensive low-incidence provision;

- regional structures would provide a channel for two-way communication between local and central government; regional groups could contribute to national data on SEN and enable us to monitor the national picture.

8 A Regional Development Agencies Bill will be introduced in the current session of Parliament, preceded by a White Paper. In carrying forward our proposals for regional arrangements for SEN we will take account of these developments and also of the role of local regeneration partnerships, funded through the Single Regeneration Budget.

QUESTION: What should be the core functions of regional planning arrangements for SEN, and how should such arrangements be set up?

Planning: the school dimension

Community special schools

9   Within the new schools framework, described in *Excellence in schools*, all maintained special schools are likely to become community special schools. This is because of the importance we attach to the place of special schools in a unified service supporting greater inclusion.

10   At present, many details of the provision made by special schools have to be specifically approved by the Secretary of State. Similarly, any change to the approved arrangements has to be decided centrally. **We propose to end this requirement for community special schools.** Detailed arrangements for more devolved decision making were described in a consultation paper on the new school framework in August. Each LEA would set up a school organisation committee to agree a local school organisation plan and to decide school organisation proposals. In drawing up their plan, LEAs would have regard to the regional plans for SEN proposed above. In deciding proposals, school organisation committees would have regard to guidance from the Secretary of State. This would reflect our policy of increasing inclusion and cover issues such as:

- the relationship between regional plans, local school organisation plans and LEA Education Development Plans;

- advice on age ranges and types of SEN which could be catered for within the same school; the appropriateness of mixed/single sex provision; and perhaps updated guidance on teaching group sizes, staffing levels and qualifications;

- delivery of the National Curriculum;

- inspection arrangements: OFSTED would monitor the extent to which LEAs took account of this guidance in organising special schools.

Non-maintained special schools and independent schools

11   Non-maintained special schools and independent schools catering wholly or mainly for children with SEN offer specialised, often residential, provision. In many cases, they make a unique contribution. Like maintained schools, they will need to take account of the developing context set out in this Green Paper. We believe therefore that this key sector should be represented in the regional planning arrangements proposed above. Where a regional plan suggests a case for establishment

of a new school, a contribution from a voluntary body, charity or private provider should be considered sympathetically.

12   All non-maintained special schools have to be specifically approved by the Secretary of State and inspected by OFSTED. We do not intend to change these arrangements.

13   Independent schools providing for SEN are subject to three specific controls:

* they may seek approval by the Secretary of State: LEAs are then free to place pupils with statements in them within the terms of the approval. Otherwise LEAs may place children with statements in independent schools only with the case by case consent of the Secretary of State;

* they are subject to inspection. Schools which have been approved are inspected by OFSTED on a 4-yearly cycle (from 1998, 6-yearly). Other independent schools are inspected by HMI. We propose to ensure that independent schools providing specifically for children with SEN, but which have not received the Secretary of State's approval, are inspected at least every 5 years and that the inspection reports are published; and

* residential schools are subject to inspections by social services departments under the Children Act.

Changes to the arrangements for independent schools

14   The number of applications for consent to place individual children with a statement at non-approved independent schools has risen sharply: the Secretary of State currently receives over 700 applications a year. It is questionable whether it is appropriate for decisions to be taken centrally on this scale about the suitability of a particular school for a particular child. The arrangement also blurs LEAs' accountability for their decisions about placement. Yet it is essential that the children at these schools, many of them very vulnerable, should be well-served and that these expensive placements should offer value for money. We want to safeguard and improve standards in education and care.

15   *We therefore propose to retain approval for independent schools, but to end the current consent arrangements.* Approval would be a clear mark of good standing. Schools would be encouraged to work towards it. LEAs would not need consent to place a child with a statement at an

independent school outside the approved list, but would have an unambiguous responsibility to satisfy themselves that placement at such a school was appropriate and in the child's interest.

16   LEAs would be required to obtain available written reports on the school from OFSTED (or OHMCI for placements in Wales), social services departments for residential schools and any association of independent schools to which the school belonged. We should also expect them to visit the school in advance of placement to satisfy themselves that it could provide for the child's special needs including, where necessary, therapeutic or medical input; and to review the placement regularly. Placements would be monitored by HMI.

QUESTION: What changes are needed to the existing arrangements for the placement of children with SEN in independent schools?

SUMMARY

By 2002...

- Regional planning machinery for SEN will be in place across England, helping to co-ordinate provision for low-incidence disabilities, specialist teacher training and other aspects of SEN.

- There will be clear guidance to support the effective development of special schools in the context of a policy of increased inclusion.

- New arrangements will be in place to safeguard the interests of children with special educational needs who are placed in independent schools.

6 Developing skills

Professional development – for teachers and others – will be needed if staff are to have the skills, knowledge and understanding to make a reality of our proposals for raising standards for all children with special educational needs.

The mainstream context

1   The success of our proposals will depend in large measure on how far they are reflected in the work of mainstream schools. Headteachers of mainstream schools usually delegate responsibility for overseeing the day-to-day operation of a school's SEN policy to the SEN co-ordinator (or SENCO). The SENCO oversees the school's provision for SEN, including the work of learning support assistants (LSAs), advises and supports fellow teachers, and liaises with parents. The SENCO also contributes to the in-service training of school staff.

Case study

The role of SENCOs

Last year, Newcastle University undertook a research project into the effective management of the SENCO role. This showed that, despite some continuing concerns, many SENCOs had found that their initial anxieties about the demands of the role had given way to increasing familiarity and confidence. In particular, SENCOs broadly endorsed the Code's underlying principle of responding quickly, professionally and effectively to pupils' difficulties so that all children had access to educational experiences of the highest quality.

The findings of this research and of other projects on individual education plans and school SEN policies were incorporated in *The SENCO Guide*, published by the DfEE and issued to schools in September 1997.

2   But a SENCO cannot do everything single-handedly. It is the responsibility of *all* teachers and support staff in a school

- to be aware of the school's responsibilities for children with special educational needs;

- to have regard to the guidance in the Code of Practice;

- to apply that guidance effectively in assessing and teaching children with SEN; and

- to work together in the classroom to raise standards for *all* pupils.

3   A 'whole school approach' is therefore essential. This will be possible only if teachers and other staff are confident that they can support children's special needs, and are familiar with the key principles of the Code of Practice. To ensure that they have this confidence, schools must develop a clear policy on SEN, communicate it to all staff, and monitor and review it regularly. In all this, it is important for the school's senior management team and governors to work with and support the SENCO.

Professional development of teachers

4   *Excellence in schools* made clear our commitment to giving trainee teachers, new entrants to the profession and those already in teaching the training and support they need to raise standards. Training in special educational needs is a priority, whether teachers work in mainstream or special schools or in LEA support services. We welcome the inclusion of the SEN dimension in the Teacher Training Agency's (TTA's) work on developing professional standards for teachers. The TTA's SEN Focus Group will liaise closely with the new National Advisory Group on SEN.

Initial teacher training (ITT) and induction

5   We have announced new standards which all trainee teachers will be expected to reach in order to qualify. These include standards in special needs training which mean that all newly qualified teachers (NQTs) will:

- understand their responsibilities under the Code of Practice;

- be capable of identifying children with special educational needs;

- be able to differentiate teaching practice appropriately.

The TTA is encouraging the development of initial teacher training courses which, while meeting our new requirements for all ITT courses, contain a greater emphasis on SEN. Best practice in training new teachers to teach children with SEN will be disseminated to ITT providers more widely. In addition, the new employment based routes leading to Qualified Teacher Status allow trainee teachers to gain experience in special schools if they wish.

6   The introduction of a supported induction year, announced in *Excellence in schools*, will allow newly qualified teachers to consolidate their skills in relation to the standards for NQTs, and to identify further development needs. SENCOs will have an important role in providing specialist support to new teachers during their first year.

Continuing professional development

7   We will encourage all teachers to develop further skills in curriculum planning, teaching and assessing pupils with SEN. Some LEAs are well placed to oversee a general staff development policy for SEN – identifying the training needs of generalist and specialist teachers in schools in the area and co-ordinating training and development programmes. But smaller authorities and those which do not have a support service infrastructure for delivering SEN training may have a more limited capacity for this. All authorities will benefit from drawing on the widest possible range of expertise.

8   ***We will therefore encourage partnerships in teacher training.*** Chapter 5 suggests that regional planning arrangements might help LEAs and higher education institutions work together, to identify training needs and provide qualified staff, particularly for low-incidence needs. LEAs should collaborate with higher education institutions in providing programmes of training for serving teachers. Health authorities, too, will have a part to play. We intend, as resources permit, to expand the current programme for SEN teacher training. We expect to encourage regional planning and co-operation by channelling funding preferentially to collaborative schemes.

QUESTION: How can we promote partnerships in in-service teacher training to raise the level of teachers' expertise in meeting special educational needs?

Headteachers

9   The TTA has produced national standards for headteachers, covering such aspects of strategic leadership and accountability as:

- monitoring and evaluating the quality of teaching, standards of learning and achievement of all pupils, including those with special educational needs;

- setting and meeting targets for improvement; and

- motivating and enabling teachers, including SENCOs, to develop their expertise through continuing professional development.

These standards are reflected in the National Professional Qualification for Headship recently launched by the TTA, and in the programme for serving headteachers currently being developed.

Special educational needs co-ordinators (SENCOs)

10   We welcome the TTA's consultation on national standards for SENCOs, which will set clear expectations and provide a focus for training. All SENCOs, with the support of their senior management and governing body, will be expected to work towards the standards, once these have been agreed. In principle it would be possible to develop the standards further, as the basis for a qualification.

QUESTION: Should the Teacher Training Agency's work on national standards be taken forward as the basis for a qualification for SEN co-ordinators?

SEN specialists

11   The skills of SEN specialists – staff in special schools, units in mainstream schools, pupil referral units, and LEA support services – need to be developed to meet the increasingly complex range of children's needs and the variety of settings in which they are educated. We are keen to review the arrangements for specialist training for these teachers. Over time, this might lead to a qualification which could replace the current mandatory and other qualifications in SEN. This could combine generic elements with components focused on more specific areas of SEN, and would give recognition to teachers who have acquired the professional skills to meet particular types of special needs. Above all, linked to clear expectations of the skills needed in different settings, it would promote high standards of provision for children with complex SEN.

QUESTION: Should there be national standards and/or a qualification for other SEN specialists?

Learning support assistants (LSAs)

12   Learning support assistants (LSAs) have many different job titles across the country. They are non-teaching assistants employed to work with children with SEN in mainstream and special schools. Their tasks include helping pupils with reading difficulties, supporting speech therapy programmes, and helping pupils to access the curriculum.

13   In January 1997 over 24,000 LSAs (full-time equivalent) were working in mainstream primary and secondary schools in England. Almost 16,000 LSAs were in maintained special schools. Numbers have risen sharply in

recent years, probably in response to the increase in the number of pupils with statements being educated in mainstream schools.

14   The contribution of LSAs is central to successful SEN practice in mainstream and special schools. The reliance which many schools place on LSAs makes training and career development essential. But training opportunities and patterns of employment are patchy, and need to be improved if we are to realise the full potential of their contribution.

15   OFSTED has found that fewer than half of LEAs provide appropriate training for learning support staff. Some LEAs have, however, developed accredited courses with higher education institutions and Training and Enterprise Councils. Health authorities may also have an important role in training LSAs to support children with substantial and complex difficulties, including "medical" needs.

Case study

Training for special needs assistants in Tower Hamlets

Tower Hamlets LEA, in partnership with its schools, has worked with the London East Training and Enterprise Council (LETEC) to develop a one term training course for special needs assistants. Participants must have been registered unemployed for at least six months or be returners to work; often they have been working on a voluntary basis in schools. The course gives trainees the practical skills and knowledge needed to help children with SEN in mainstream classrooms. It focuses on support strategies for a range of different needs, on encouraging children to become independent and on developing their self-esteem. Participants spend two half days a week in schools, supervised by a teacher. About 90% are successful in finding work after completing the course.

The LEA has also been working with UNISON on an open learning course, *Return to Learn*, which will give special needs assistants an opportunity to improve their study skills. During the ten month course, which is accredited through the National Open College Network, participants explore areas of writing and analysing and working with figures. Personal tutors provide feedback and advice, and a study group encourages participants to learn together. LETEC funding will make it possible to offer assistants day-time release to attend this course. It is hoped that participants will use the course as a stepping stone to higher level courses, such as the Open University Specialist Teacher Assistant Certificate.

16 Where LEAs are the employers of LSAs, or hold a register of LSAs on which schools draw, it is easier to offer structured training. The involvement of the LEA also makes possible greater continuity in employment, and so increases the extent to which expertise can be built up. But LSAs' careers might be enhanced by a national structure including some or all of the following:

- national guidelines or a framework of good practice for LEAs and schools to follow;

- an expectation that LEAs would make available accredited training for all LSAs and oversee quality assurance;

- nationally devised modules for all LSA training courses within an NVQ framework – perhaps including a mandatory induction/foundation course, with additional modules to reflect the needs of pupils.

17 *Excellence in schools* said that we would consult LEAs about developing a programme of courses and qualifications for all non-teaching assistants. Training for LSAs would form part of that programme. At the same time, training for teachers needs to equip them to work with other adults in the classroom.

QUESTION: What action should we take to improve the training and career structure of learning support assistants?

School governors

18 A fundamental objective for governing bodies is to help raise standards. Monitoring the school's arrangements for children with SEN is part and parcel of that. In addition, governors have statutory responsibilities to publish information in their annual report about the school's SEN policy

and about the school's admissions arrangements for pupils with disabilities, including how the school will help such pupils gain access and what it will do to make sure they are treated fairly. Governors should therefore be actively involved in developing, supporting, and reviewing the school's policy on SEN in consultation with the headteacher and SENCO. Yet OFSTED's report on the Code in 1996 commented that many governors were not aware of their responsibilities for SEN.

19 Opportunities for high quality training in special needs for governors should be improved. *Excellence in schools* committed us to issuing guidance on how governors' training needs can be met, drawing on the best of existing LEA practice; this guidance will cover governors' responsibilities for pupils with SEN.

QUESTION: What kinds of training would help governors to carry out effectively their responsibilities for pupils with SEN?

Educational psychologists

20 Educational psychologists (EPs) employed by LEAs have wide responsibilities. But a large part of their time is tied up in the process of statutory assessment. While this may be necessary in some cases, it diverts key resources from early intervention and from providing help and support to pupils when it is most needed. **We will explore ways of changing the balance of work of EPs, so that they can use their expertise as productively as possible.**

21 More effective support at the school-based stages of the Code, with EPs and LEA learning support staff spending more time working in schools, should mean that, over time, there will be less demand for statutory assessments. Furthermore, it may be that as the skills of SENCOs and other SEN staff develop, they could, with suitable training, perform some aspects of statutory assessment, so releasing EPs for other tasks.

22 Changes in the balance of work of EPs will have implications for their training. New patterns of training will be needed to reflect their developing role in areas such as strategic management, working with schools, curriculum issues and family therapy.

QUESTION: What changes are needed in the role and training of educational psychologists?

SUMMARY

By 2002...

- There will be a clear structure for teachers' professional development in SEN, from a strengthened attention to SEN issues in initial training through to improved training for headteachers, SEN co-ordinators and other SEN specialists.

- There will be a national framework for training learning support assistants.

- There will be national guidance on training governors to carry out their responsibilities for pupils with SEN.

- There will be national agreement on ways of reducing the time spent by educational psychologists on statutory assessments and maximising their contribution in the classroom, and the training necessary for their developing role.

7 *Working together*

The Government, LEAs, other local agencies and business need to work together in supporting the education of children with SEN. Their contributions need to be developed, improved and co-ordinated to achieve our aims of raising standards, shifting resources to practical support and increasing inclusion.

Government

1   The Government has a central responsibility for raising standards and promoting progress for all children, including those with SEN. We are responsible for the framework of national SEN policy within which schools and LEAs operate, and for monitoring its effectiveness. We also support schools and LEAs by:

- communicating with them, through visits and contacts at many levels, and providing information: DfEE's Special Educational Needs Division is the main channel for communication;

- identifying and disseminating good practice, for example:

  - by commissioning research on aspects of SEN or including an SEN dimension in other commissioned research;

  - through published guidance from the Standards and Effectiveness Unit, which is working towards establishing a database of best practice nationally;

  - through OFSTED inspection data and HMI surveys; and

  - by encouraging teacher groups, local and national organisations and schools to exchange information using the Internet;

- collecting and publishing statistical information;

- encouraging benchmarking; and

- ensuring that co-ordination between Government Departments secures mutually-reinforcing policies towards children with SEN.

In carrying out these functions we will look to the National Advisory Group on SEN to advise on the development and implementation of policies to improve standards in education for children with SEN.

Research into and dissemination of information about good practice

2   Some ways of meeting children's special educational needs are demonstrably more effective than others. ***We will promote research designed to establish good practice, and disseminate the results.*** The areas to be covered might range from ways of meeting the needs of children with autism to working with learning support assistants in the classroom. Such research will supplement the information available in specialist journals and from voluntary bodies and LEAs.

3   It is however very difficult for busy teachers, LEA administrators and others to keep up with all this information, and to assess its relevance to their own circumstances. One way of disseminating reliable and objective information about good practice in SEN would be to establish a small national institute to sift evidence from other sources and target the conclusions to SENCOs, other specialist teachers, SEN governors and LEA administrators. Such an institute should principally be funded by subscription, from LEAs, schools and others, who felt access to a research digest of this type would help them to improve the effectiveness of their provision for SEN.

4   Whether or not such arrangements are established nationally, we shall continue to join in relevant international projects. In particular, we shall play a leading part in the new European Agency for Development in Special Needs Education. This has as its aim the dissemination of information, chiefly over the Internet, about special needs provision in 17 European countries. We welcome the initiative of the Danish authorities in establishing the Agency, and will ensure that its output is available to schools and others in this country.

QUESTION: What arrangements would help the speedy dissemination of useful information about good practice in SEN?

Co-operation between local agencies

5   Effective collaboration between LEAs, social services departments and health authorities is essential. Too often the fragmentation of services between different statutory agencies, competition and tight budgets has left parents to take responsibility for co-ordinating provision for their child.

6   The need for closer co-operation starts in Government. The National Advisory Group on SEN includes people with expertise in education, health and social services. We will work towards effective co-ordination of policy for young children in these areas by strengthening links between the DfEE and the Department of Health. The Departments are, for example, jointly funding a research project on inter-agency co-operation based at Newcastle University. A Green Paper on the Government's health strategy, to be published later this year, will consult on targets for redressing inequality in the health of children and young people, which has clear links to social competence and educational achievement.

7   Effective collaboration between statutory agencies is particularly important for those children with SEN who are defined by the Children Act as being "in need", including those looked after by local authorities. Some local authorities undertake joint planning and funding of residential educational placements or packages of care for children in need. The regional planning arrangements discussed in Chapter 5 may encourage such practices to become more widespread. Sir William Utting's imminent report on safeguards for children living away from home will have an important bearing on these and related matters in this Green Paper. Where children looked after by a local authority are placed in a residential special school, the placement should be jointly planned and funded by the education and social services departments and, where appropriate, the health authority. In working together, statutory agencies should also involve local voluntary bodies to the maximum extent possible.

QUESTION: **What are the barriers to improved collaboration between LEAs, social services departments and health authorities? How can these be overcome?**

Provision of speech and language therapy

8   One area where collaboration needs to be improved is speech and language therapy. This is a key to raising the educational potential of children with communication difficulties. Communication skills are in turn a pre-requisite for literacy skills. When communication problems persist into school years the greatest benefits can be achieved where speech therapists work with teachers and other staff as part of a team, monitoring the progress of children regularly. *We will consider funding joint research by the DfEE and the Department of Health into the factors which lead to the most effective provision of speech and language therapy for children.* Our proposal to end the distinction between educational and non-educational needs and provision in statements (see Chapter 3) will be relevant.

9   Children with communication difficulties have a right to a thorough assessment, effective support and regular reviews of progress. There are examples of collaboration between agencies and schools, but in too many cases provision of speech and language therapy to children has been hindered by the conflicting duties and powers of health authorities and LEAs and by lack of clarity over funding. *We will look at these obstacles, and if necessary change the law so that children receive the service they need.*

10　In 1991, changes were introduced to the way speech and language therapy services were provided in Scotland to school-aged children. These changes gave education authorities direct control over the financial resources they needed to discharge their duties towards children with the equivalent of a statement. Education authorities now purchase these therapy services direct from health authorities. This model has been suggested as one which might help resolve the difficulties in England.

11　Another approach would be for LEAs and health authorities to have joint responsibility for funding and managing speech and language therapy services for all children. Recognising the benefits of early intervention in communication difficulties, health authorities and LEAs could make sure that speech and language therapy was co-ordinated for pre-school children, and continued smoothly into primary school for those children with the most persistent difficulties.

12　Similar issues apply with other therapies. We will consider whether any changes to the provision of speech therapy should be extended to cover the arrangements for the funding of physiotherapy and occupational therapy. We will also consider whether any other services, such as mobility training for visually impaired children or provision of school nurses, would benefit from better collaboration.

QUESTION: How should funding for speech and language therapy and analogous services be provided in future?

Transition from school to further and higher education, training or employment

13　LEAs, social services departments, health authorities and careers services need to work together in transition planning as pupils with SEN come to the end of their compulsory schooling. We will encourage these agencies to co-operate to give priority to this work, and see that transition planning starts early. The review of the Code of Practice proposed in Chapter 3 will consider whether aspects of the existing arrangements can be improved.

Case study

Oxfordshire Integrated Assessment Project

The Oxfordshire Joint Commissioning Reference Group for Children with Disabilities has commissioned a two-year project to provide an integrated assessment for young people who will probably have support needs in adulthood. The project is now in its main pilot phase, with 26 young people and their families participating.

At 14+, the integrated assessment incorporates a number of features to assist planning by adult and further education services:

- the first annual review of a statement after the young person's 14th birthday, and the subsequent transition plan;

- an assessment by social services under the Disabled Persons Act 1996; and

- an assessment by adult (health and social) services of the future needs of a young person with disabilities who may require support from medical or social services.

After the education transition plan has been completed, social services care managers work with the young person and their family to produce a future needs plan and action checklist. Together, these record what needs to be done, and who is responsible. The checklist is used by parents and professionals. The aim is for the different agencies to develop together a plan for the young person's transition to adulthood.

14 LEAs and schools also need to work with colleges to help pupils with SEN move on to further and higher education. Many successfully make the transition, often helped through school/college link courses. But improvements are needed so that more can do so. There are some gaps in post-school provision for students with the most severe and complex needs. The Further Education Funding Council's (FEFC) study *Mapping Provision* and statistical returns from schools show that the proportion of

pupils with SEN in secondary schools is higher than the proportion of students with learning difficulties and/or disabilities in further education. A lack of reliable information on the routes pupils with SEN take when they leave school makes these figures difficult to interpret. It is also unclear how far young people's decisions are affected by the fact that statements may remain in force for 16-19-year-olds in school, but not in FE. *We propose to study ways of evaluating the post-school experiences of young people who have been identified at school as having SEN.*

15   Opportunities for students with learning difficulties and/or disabilities in further education will be improved through implementation of the recommendations of the FEFC's report *Inclusive Learning* (the "Tomlinson report"). The National Committee of Inquiry into Higher Education looked at increasing participation and widening access to higher education. We are currently considering our response to its recommendations.

16   Support from business can have a major impact in preparing young people, including those with SEN, for adult and working life. *Excellence in schools* set out our proposals for adding a new drive to school-business links. Such links can motivate and develop the skills of young people with SEN, encouraging them to see themselves as future employees.

17   Employment opportunities for young people with special needs will be improved through our Welfare to Work programme. Through this programme and our planned Millennium Volunteers programme we will explore options for disabled young adults to help in schools, and so assist in creating a positive approach to disability.

18   A forthcoming White Paper will set out our policies and plans for all post-16 lifelong learning issues. Our vision is of a learning society; one where *all* people have access to lifelong learning.

QUESTION: **How can we help more young people with SEN make a successful transition to further or higher education, training and employment?**

SUMMARY

By 2002...

- There will be new arrangements for disseminating up-to-date information about good practice in SEN provision.

- There will be improved co-operation and co-ordination between local education authorities, social services departments and health authorities, with the focus on meeting children's special needs more effectively.

- Speech and language therapy will be provided more effectively for children who need it.

- The Department will be collecting information about the experiences, once they have left school, of young people with SEN, to help schools and colleges prepare young people for adult life more effectively.

8 Principles into practice: emotional and behavioural difficulties

We want to put our principles into practice for all children with SEN, including one group which presents schools with special challenges – children with emotional and behavioural difficulties. The number of children perceived as falling within this group is increasing. We need to find ways of tackling their difficulties early, before they lead to under-achievement, disaffection and, in too many cases, exclusion from mainstream education.

Children with emotional and behavioural difficulties: a strategy for action

1   This chapter exemplifies the policies and action proposed in the rest of this Green Paper for one group of children: those with "emotional and behavioural difficulties" (EBD). This term is applied to a broad range of young people – preponderantly boys – with a very wide spectrum of needs, from those with short term emotional difficulties to those with extremely challenging behaviour or serious psychological difficulties. Defining this group is not easy; difficulties are compounded by the fact that different agencies often use different terminology. For schools, pupils with EBD can present problems to which exclusion has sometimes seemed the only recourse. Even where they are not formally excluded, many of these children effectively remove themselves from the educational process. Children with EBD are at great risk of under-achievement, educationally and in their personal development. They can also disrupt the education of others.

2   The roots of EBD are complex. They include family disadvantage or breakdown, poor parenting skills and poor experiences at school. Emotional difficulties may lead to poor behaviour, and should therefore be addressed as early as possible. The emotional well-being of all children will be highlighted in the forthcoming Green Paper on the Government's health strategy. In some instances EBD may stem from other special educational needs.

3   This chapter does not seek to analyse in detail the different ways in which the term EBD is used. But we recognise that distinctions matter in practice. The wide variation of needs and causes is reflected in a wide range of different provision. Some of this, for various reasons, is not improving children's performance; failure and disaffection are increasingly marked as they approach Key Stage 4. Improving the quality of provision for young people identified as having EBD, and preventing other children from manifesting such difficulties, is one of the most urgent, and one of the most daunting, tasks facing schools.

4   Tackling EBD is therefore one area in which, over time, we aim to shift resources from remedial action to preventive work. Placements in EBD special schools are expensive. The cost to society more widely of failure to tackle these problems is higher still, both in terms of reduced economic contribution in adult life and, for some, of criminal activity and prison.

5   We do not expect schools to solve, unaided, problems which are linked to wider social issues. There needs to be the closest co-operation between the education service and other agencies. And there needs to be co-ordinated action at school, local and national levels. For example, schools should be looking at the full range of policies and practices which affect the way in which their pupils behave. LEAs will be consulting schools on the contents of local behaviour support plans. At national level we need to look at financial and other incentives for good practice, and possibly at national targets (for example, for reduced numbers of exclusions).

6   Within such a framework, we believe that the foundations for an overall strategy are:

- education policies for improving the achievement of all children, combined with broader social policies to combat disadvantage;

- early identification and intervention, with schools and other agencies working with the families of children with EBD;

- effective behaviour policies in schools and LEAs;

- strengthening the skills of all staff working with pupils with EBD;

- a range of specialist support to meet the varied needs of pupils within this broad group;

- wider dissemination of existing best practice; and

- encouraging fresh approaches in the secondary years.

We shall welcome views on this strategy. We are pleased that the National Advisory Group on SEN has set up a sub-group – its first – to examine ways of improving provision for pupils with EBD. The sub-group will consider views expressed in response to this chapter, and will take them into account in advising on a programme for action which will build on the approaches described below.

Improving achievement

7   The full range of policies for improving performance in basic skills and for working with parents, summarised in Chapters 1 and 2, should help to forestall the emergence of emotional and behavioural difficulties in many children who might develop EBD as a consequence of early failure at school. More broadly still, our policies for a fairer society combine an emphasis on individual responsibility with real opportunities. They will not

bring about an immediate transformation. But they will begin to create a social climate which engenders hope, not disaffection.

Early identification and intervention

8 Early intervention can be particularly successful in tackling EBD. Some of the measures described in Chapter 1 will be especially relevant. Sound assessment is the first step: boundaries between EBD, ordinary unruliness, disaffection and various clinical conditions are not always clear-cut but have a major bearing on the solution required. A number of assessment techniques are already in use. ***We will be prepared to support the development and wider dissemination of these.***

9 The priority must be to help schools and LEA support services improve the performance of these children. In most cases schools find that using the framework of the Code of Practice – described in Chapter 3 – helps them to tackle children's behavioural problems in a systematic way. For children with more complex difficulties, there are some promising models for intervention in the primary years. These exemplify the collaborative approaches discussed in Chapter 7, with key roles for social services departments, health authorities and parents. ***The DfEE and the Department of Health will work together to establish a national programme of early intervention projects for nursery and primary age children identified as having EBD.***

Case study

Nurture groups in Enfield

In Enfield, some primary schools run nurture groups for children showing early signs of emotional and behavioural difficulties. These small special classes provide a structured and predictable environment in which the children can begin to trust adults and to learn. Careful consideration is given to appropriate curriculum content. The nurture groups are an integral part of Enfield schools' mainstream provision for children with special educational needs. The LEA's advisory staff and educational psychology service support and train the nurture group teachers and assistants. Parents are regularly involved in discussions about their child's progress and attend informal sessions. Pupils are

> encouraged to take part in school activities including assemblies and playtimes. Many pupils are able to function wholly in a mainstream class within a year.

Inclusion: effective behaviour policies

10 Applying to children with EBD the policies on inclusion in Chapter 4 will present mainstream schools with sharp challenges. But the factors which enable some schools to respond successfully to these challenges are becoming clear. Schools need to offer a setting where *all* children are valued and encouraged to behave well, where there are clear guidelines for behaviour, teaching is positive, and where damaged self-esteem can be rebuilt. Many are working towards whole school strategies designed to sustain this approach, encompassing pastoral systems, specific policies to promote achievement by boys, and explicit agreement about the role of support services. Such approaches need the support of all staff, and a strong lead from the school's management. The proposals in *Excellence in schools* to encourage the careful introduction of "assertive discipline", and for home-school contracts, will have a part to play in helping many schools to establish a basic approach. **We shall consider how to promote good practice in providing for EBD in mainstream schools, drawing on a project being carried out by the University of Birmingham with DfEE funding.**

11 This will be a developing process. The handling of exclusions will be central to it. The QCA is carrying out a project exploring curriculum factors leading to the exclusion of children with EBD. Too often, an excluded child (especially one labelled as having EBD) enters a cycle from which they never return to the mainstream. The direction in which we should move is clear: all schools should be helped to take responsibility for all their pupils. All should be taking positive action to reduce to a minimum the number of permanent exclusions. But to do so they need practical support from the LEA. In some cases, schools and LEAs should consider establishing (or re-establishing) in-school units which can address children's problems without breaking the link with mainstream schooling.

Case study

Langdon School, Newham

Langdon School, Newham, is an inclusive, mixed, multi-cultural school with over 1,800 students. It includes young people with a wide range of special educational needs including those with moderate or severe learning difficulties and emotional and behavioural difficulties.

The number of children with SEN at the school has increased in recent years. Yet fixed term exclusions have fallen significantly and there have been no permanent exclusions from the school for over two years. At the same time pupils' performance in GCSE examinations has improved.

These benefits have been achieved through:

- a review of the school's policies and practices for behaviour management;

- whole school staff training focusing on teaching and learning styles, including differentiation of the curriculum and strategies for behaviour management in the classroom;

- development of a tightly networked pastoral system, using approaches such as peer mediation, mentoring and outreach work;

- partnership with the LEA's Behavioural Support Service, working in the school to prevent exclusions; and

- working with local primary schools well before children move to Langdon School.

12   From April 1998 LEAs will be required to prepare behaviour support plans setting out their arrangements for the education of children with behavioural difficulties, including those with special educational needs. These will provide a framework for all relevant services, from support for mainstream schools through to specialist provision. We will be consulting widely this

autumn on guidance on the preparation of behaviour support plans. This will emphasise the importance of effective co-ordination between local agencies and of ensuring that behaviour support plans dovetail with Children's Services Plans and other relevant activities, such as the work of the proposed Youth Offender Teams on, for example, Final Warnings. We will also be consulting on whether greater use can be made of financial incentives to encourage schools to keep pupils at risk of exclusion and to admit pupils who have previously been excluded from other schools.

Case study

Effective behaviour policies

Newtown Primary School, Carlisle

Newtown Primary School is situated on an estate with a shifting population suffering from social deprivation and problem behaviour. The school has a high proportion of children on its SEN register. There had been a history of disruptive behaviour. The headteacher and staff saw the need for a clear and consistent behaviour policy, and decided that the key to improving behaviour was to address the children's low self-esteem.

Together the staff developed a merit system to celebrate pupils' achievements and good behaviour; pupils are rewarded with certificates, badges and stickers at a weekly assembly. Working alongside this is a 'traffic lights' system for unacceptable behaviour. Children start each session on green and move through amber and red if, following inappropriate behaviour, they fail to respond to teachers' verbal prompts. A child on red begins to build up time which has to be repaid at playtime or lunch before the child can return to green. The school has successfully applied its behaviour policy – backed up by clear and consistent explanations about why certain behaviour is inappropriate – and the number of exclusions has fallen. The school's OFSTED inspection report (March 1997) described Newtown as a school "characterised by good behaviour".

The school recognises the importance of parental support in motivating children to learn. Newtown encourages parents to become involved in their children's education by welcoming them to breakfast and homework clubs. The school is also running a trial parent support club which includes a family literacy programme.

Highfield Junior School, Plymouth

Over the past five years Highfield Junior School has introduced a new code of discipline to promote positive behaviour in the school. Initiatives like circle time underline the school's belief that pupils should be offered ownership of the system in which they work and a say in what goes on. During circle time, the children gather in a circle on the floor and concentrate their discussion on one specific idea or concept. They talk one at a time and listen carefully to each other.

Circle time is used regularly in classes in the following ways:

- to build up group rapport and individuals' self-esteem;

- to identify, as a class, the needs and strengths of all members;

- to offer solutions, care support and strategies to the individual or group when a problem such as bullying arises;

- to solve disputes through group discussion;

- to accelerate a whole school approach to policy development in matters such as behaviour management and school rules.

Staff have been pleased with the way in which pupils apply a circle time approach to their personal problem solving and decision making; and are convinced that standards of learning and ability have improved as a result.

Strengthening staff skills

13   Teachers need to be helped to develop their skills in working with children with EBD, to forestall problems where possible and to keep to a minimum demands for specialist support. The new standards for newly qualified

teachers make it clear that all teachers should be able to deal effectively with basic classroom management and behavioural issues. Headteachers and senior staff need training and guidance on how to put in place behaviour policies. Chapter 6 proposes action to promote SEN issues in initial, induction and in-service training. Within the framework of behaviour support plans, LEAs will set out the training available to help staff manage pupil behaviour more effectively.

14   A survey by the Teacher Training Agency of SEN training has found few training opportunities for specialist staff working with pupils with EBD. Enhancing the skills of these staff is central to addressing the needs of children with severe behavioural difficulties. *We will ensure that the development of such training is a priority for the regional arrangements described in Chapter 5.*

QUESTION: **What should the DfEE do to support teachers, in mainstream and special schools, working with children with emotional and behavioural difficulties?**

Specialist support

15   Most behavioural difficulties should be dealt with in mainstream settings. An LEA's behaviour support team may have a large part to play in making this possible, both by spreading good practice and by providing targeted support for certain children. Where specific intervention is needed, there should be clear objectives and a clear plan for disengagement. The aim should always be for the school to resume full responsibility for the child.

16   As Chapter 4 acknowledges, where children's difficulties are severe, they may need – at least for a time – to be educated outside mainstream schools, in some cases in residential provision, both in their own interests and in the interests of other children. With reductions in the number of residential special schools and increased numbers of small LEAs, children with a wide range of behaviours are being educated together in all-purpose EBD schools. Providing for this wide range of needs has often proved difficult within a small school. The regional planning mechanisms suggested in Chapter 5 should make it possible to improve the match between provision and needs. Furthermore, the aim should be for children to return to a mainstream setting as soon as they are ready to do so. This will not be possible for all, but experience from other countries, including the United States, suggests that it could happen much more frequently

than at present. EBD special schools would then, like other special schools, begin to develop a broader role in providing support to mainstream schools.

Disseminating best practice

17   One of the responsibilities which we have accepted in Chapter 7 is for the identification and dissemination of good practice. EBD special schools face quite exceptional challenges. Some meet these challenges superbly. But OFSTED has found that an unacceptably high proportion of these schools fail to provide an adequate standard of teaching and learning. There is a growing body of inspection and research-based evidence which the DfEE will use to run workshops, with the support of OFSTED, on effective practice in EBD special schools. ***We shall build on these workshops to develop a programme offering consultancy support to EBD special schools.*** We shall invite some of the heads of EBD schools which have been found by OFSTED to be making outstanding provision for their pupils to take part in such a programme. Next year HMI will publish a report highlighting effective practice in EBD schools.

Encouraging fresh approaches in the secondary years

18   Similarly, we want to work with others to find ways of tackling the under-achievement of many youngsters with EBD as they approach the end of compulsory schooling. One approach might be to encourage wider use of pupil referral units (PRUs) with expertise in aspects of EBD to work in partnership with schools where such pupils are at risk of exclusion or, where they have been permanently excluded, to secure their reintegration into mainstream schooling. Our purpose would not be to constitute special schools by another name. But a targeted service of this kind might help reduce the number of pupils at risk of failure on account of poor behaviour. Closer links with mainstream schools would also help more PRUs to ensure reasonable curriculum coverage and to give priority to the aim of reintegration.

19   There is also a view that many children with EBD, including some of those in special schools, would be better provided for at lower cost through tailored programmes combining skills training, work experience and pastoral care. It is clearly sensible to consider very carefully what is known about the comparative outcomes of such programmes. The QCA is studying how to make the National Curriculum more accessible to children and young people with EBD. In particular it is looking at the most

appropriate ways of enabling schools to increase their focus on work-related education at Key Stage 4. Such a variation in curriculum and setting might improve the motivation of some young people who are disaffected with the school system and traditional curriculum and at risk of failure. Organisations such as Cities in Schools and employment related activities set up by Education Business Partnerships have shown the possibilities for renewing motivation at Key Stage 4.

Case study

Cities in Schools

Cities in Schools operates in several LEAs across England and Wales. It works principally with young people who are out of school (including special schools) because of permanent exclusion or long-term non-attendance. The majority have been in contact with outside agencies such as social services and the police, and a significant proportion have statements of SEN.

An important element of Cities in Schools' work is its Bridge Courses aimed primarily at Key Stage 4 pupils who are out of school and appear unlikely to progress to youth training, further education or employment. The courses are full-time and the weekly programme involves:

- two days at FE college focusing on basic literacy, numeracy and computer skills;

- two days work experience;

- one day working with the group tutor involving personal tutorials, group work and leisure activities.

Positive outcomes of the programme have included:

- improved attendance and attitudes towards learning;

- accreditation of literacy, numeracy and other skills;

- a high proportion of pupils moving on to further education and training.

QUESTION: **What are the most effective ways of improving provision for children with emotional and behavioural difficulties?**

SUMMARY

By 2002 ...

- A national programme will be in place to help primary schools tackle emotional and behavioural difficulties at a very early stage.

- There will be enhanced opportunities for all staff to improve their skills in teaching children with emotional and behavioural difficulties.

- There will be a national programme to offer support to EBD special schools experiencing problems.

- There will be expanded support for schemes designed to renew the motivation of young people with emotional and behavioural difficulties at Key Stage 4.

Appendix 1

Members of the National Advisory Group on SEN

Chair: Estelle Morris MP

Vice-chair: Paul Ennals	Director of Education and Employment at the Royal National Institute for the Blind and Chair of the Council for Disabled Children
Gordon Bull	Principal, Newbury College and member of FEFC's Inclusive Learning Steering Group
Clive Danks	Adviser, Special Educational Needs, Birmingham LEA
Gillian Dawson	SEN co-ordinator, Sandford Primary School, Leeds
Michael De Val	Director of Education, Torfaen County Borough Council
Prof. Alan Dyson	Special Needs Research Centre, University of Newcastle upon Tyne
Tim Exell	Headteacher, Wendover House Special School, Buckinghamshire
Chrissie Garrett	SEN co-ordinator, Banbury Secondary School, Oxfordshire and member of the Standards Task Force

Moira Gibb	Director of Social Services, Kensington and Chelsea
Paul Lincoln	Director of Education, Essex LEA
Pauline Maddison	Chief Education Services Officer, Bexley London Borough
Vincent McDonnell	Principal Education Officer, Staffordshire LEA and Chair of SEN Committee of Society of Education Officers
Kate McRae	Headteacher, Alvaston Junior Community School, Derby
Richard Rieser	Teacher, Hackney LEA, member of SEN Training Consortium's working group on teacher training for SEN and Treasurer of the National Association for SEN (Greater London Branch)
Philippa Russell OBE	Director, Council for Disabled Children
Dela Smith	Headteacher, Beaumont Hill Special School, Darlington
Sandra Tomlinson	Vice-chair, National Governors' Council
Vanessa Wiseman	Headteacher, Langdon School, Newham

Appendix 2

Funding and the SEN framework

1   One of the reasons why many parents and schools seek statutory assessments and statements is that this sometimes seems to be the only route to funding to meet children's needs. Under some approaches to delegation of school budgets, similar financial arguments can apply to the placing of pupils on particular stages of the Code of Practice.

2   *Excellence in schools* announced a new framework for Local Management of Schools (LMS). A technical consultation paper, *Framework for the Organisation of Schools*, issued in August, set out the main elements that might be included in legislation on this. We shall be consulting later this year on the detail of this new framework, including the allocation and delegation of funds to schools.

3   Many LEAs already delegate to schools the funding for all or most SEN provision at stages 1-3. In general we encourage such delegation. It means that the funding framework reflects schools' responsibilities under the Code. And it allows schools to take their own decisions about purchasing additional support, whether from their own LEA's SEN services, or from other agencies, including other LEAs or the private sector. In future the sources of such support should also include special schools. But we recognise arguments for retention by LEAs of some funding to support pupils at stages 1-3. Retention can ensure the maintenance of high quality LEA services, particularly for low incidence needs with which schools may be unfamiliar. LEAs may be best placed to promote and support increasing inclusion of pupils with SEN without the need for them always to have statements, and will have an important role in monitoring the use of delegated funding for stages 1-3. We shall welcome views on how to achieve the right balance between delegating funds to schools for functions which they can best carry out, while allowing LEAs to retain funds for functions for which they are best placed, taking account also of the regional arrangements discussed in Chapter 5.

QUESTION: What needs to be done for the new LMS arrangements to support effectively the responsibilities of both schools and LEAs for SEN provision at stages 1-3 of the Code?

4   Under the new framework, we expect to mirror LEAs' duties by proposing that funding for statutory assessments, administration and review of statements should be amongst items which LEAs can retain centrally. So would funding for provision specified in statements, but *we shall consider the arguments for promoting delegation of some of this funding, both in order to support the approaches to inclusion in Chapter 4, and for the reasons discussed below.*

5   *We will expect LEAs to review their LMS arrangements:*

   • to clarify the amount of funding delegated to schools for SEN, and

   • to eliminate features which may be acting against children's educational interests by providing purely financial incentives for statements.

6   Although funding delegated to schools is not earmarked for particular purposes, LEAs should identify explicitly for schools all the elements of delegated budgets which are related to SEN. These will usually be:

   • an element for SEN within general per pupil funding, and

   • additional funds delegated, whether through formula factors or on the basis of audit, specifically for special or additional educational needs.

   LEAs should make clear to schools the levels and types of need which they are expected to meet from their delegated budgets and what the LEA will meet from centrally retained funds. For pupils with statements, each statement should say which elements of the specified provision are to be met from the school's delegated budget, and which "extra" elements the LEA will separately fund.

7   To limit the purely financial incentives for statements, LEAs should consider the formula they use to distribute funding for SEN. The possibility of such incentives is reduced where objective proxy measures such as free school meals are used as a starting point. It may be possible to develop other such indicators, drawing for example on the results of baseline assessment. LEAs will continue to be free to base funding on the reported incidence of SEN. But where they choose this approach, they need to ensure that it does not influence assessments of children's needs.

8   LEAs should avoid large steps in funding, whether between stage 3 and statements, or between Code of Practice stages or local equivalents.

Funding arrangements should as far as possible reflect the continuum of special needs, and should not result in substantial differences in funding level where there are relatively small differences in need. Partial delegation by formula of the funding for statements might assist in establishing this continuum, although funding arrangements would need to recognise that the number of children with statements in a school, and the cost of their statements, will vary from year to year.

Appendix 3

Arrangements for consultation

Key questions

This Green Paper initiates a wide-ranging review of education for children with special educational needs. Following consultation, we intend to draw up an action plan for the remainder of this Parliament, with measures which will lead to improved provision for children with SEN. The key questions on which we would welcome comments are as follows:

Policies for excellence

1

- How can we identify children's special educational needs earlier, and ensure that appropriate intervention addresses those needs?

- What should the DfEE do to encourage and disseminate good practice in target setting for pupils with special educational needs, in both mainstream and special schools?

- How can we identify and disseminate good practice in delivering the curriculum to children with special educational needs?

- Do the existing arrangements for assessment within the National Curriculum, and for public examinations, give appropriate recognition of the achievements of children with special educational needs? If not, how might they be improved?

- What should the DfEE do to promote Information and Communications Technology as a means of supporting children with special educational needs?

Working with parents

2

- How can we make sure that parents receive the support they need at all stages of their child's education?

- How can we encourage dialogue between parents, schools and LEAs, and resolve disputes about SEN as early as possible?

- Are changes needed to improve the effectiveness of the SEN Tribunal?

Practical support: the framework for SEN provision

3

- Will it be helpful to review the Code of Practice, with a view to a revised version in 1999? If so, which aspects of the Code need particular attention? How can we reduce the paperwork associated with Code?

- How can LEAs help schools improve the quality of provision at stages 1-3 of the Code of Practice?

- How can we strengthen the assurance to parents that schools will offer effective and consistent support at stages 1-3 of the Code of Practice? Should we introduce contracts between schools and parents specifying the agreed extra provision the child will receive at stage 3?

- How might we secure greater national consistency in making statements, or in placing children at the other stages of the Code of Practice?

- What changes should be made to the contents of, or monitoring and review arrangements for, statements of SEN?

Increasing inclusion

4

- What priority measures should we take to include more pupils with special educational needs within mainstream schools?

- What should the proposed Code of Practice on admissions say about the admission of pupils with SEN?

- How can we help special schools develop their role, working more closely with mainstream schools to meet the needs of all pupils with SEN?

Planning SEN provision

5

- What should be the core functions of regional planning arrangements for SEN, and how should such arrangements be set up?

- What changes are needed to the existing arrangements for the placement of children with SEN in independent schools?

Developing Skills

6

- How can we promote partnerships in in-service teacher training to raise the level of teachers' expertise in meeting special educational needs?

- Should the Teacher Training Agency's work on national standards be taken forward as the basis for a qualification for SEN co-ordinators?

- Should there be national standards and/or a qualification for other SEN specialists?

- What action should we take to improve the training and career structure of learning support assistants?

- What kinds of training would help governors to carry out effectively their responsibilities for pupils with SEN?

- What changes are needed in the role and training of educational psychologists?

Working together

7

- What arrangements would help the speedy dissemination of useful information about good practice in SEN?

- What are the barriers to improved collaboration between LEAs, social services departments and health authorities? How can these be overcome?

- How should funding for speech and language therapy and analogous services be provided in future?

- How can we help more young people with SEN make a successful transition to further or higher education, training and employment?

Principles into practice: emotional and behavioural difficulties

8

- What should the DfEE do to support teachers, in mainstream and special schools, working with children with emotional and behavioural difficulties?

- What are the most effective ways of improving provision for children with emotional and behavioural difficulties?

Appendix 2 – Funding and the SEN framework

- What needs to be done for the new LMS arrangements to support effectively the responsibilities of both schools and LEAs for SEN provision at stages 1-3 of the Code?

Copies of the Green Paper

Copies of this Green Paper are being sent to all LEAs, headteachers, chairs of governing bodies, SEN co-ordinators and national bodies involved in the education of children with SEN.

The Green Paper is available in Braille and on audio-cassette.

A separate Green Paper will be published in Wales.

Summary version

A summary version of the Green Paper is also being sent to schools in England. Further copies of the summary version are available free of charge from:

DfEE Publications
PO Box 5050
Sudbury
SUFFOLK
CO10 6ZQ

Tel: 0845 60 222 60
Fax: 0845 60 333 60
Email: dfee@prologcs.demon.co.uk

The summary is available in Braille and on audio-cassette.

How to respond to consultation

We will be undertaking a wide-ranging consultation on the Green Paper, including regional conferences, meetings with national bodies and local meetings and discussions with parents and representatives of schools and LEAs.

We welcome comments on all the areas covered by the Green Paper, and in particular on the specific questions listed above, by **Friday 9 January 1998**. Under the *Code of Practice on Open Government*, any responses will be made available to the public on request unless respondents indicate that they wish their response to remain confidential.

Written comments should be sent to:

Alison Britton
DfEE
Special Educational Needs Division
Area 2T
Sanctuary Buildings
Great Smith Street
LONDON SW1P 3BT

Tel: 0171 925 5971
Fax: 0171 925 6986

Internet

The Green Paper and its summary version are available on the Internet. The address is **http://www.open.gov.uk/dfee/dfeehome.htm**. Comments can be emailed to **dfee.sen@gtnet.gov.uk**.

If you would like to discuss any of the issues raised in the Green Paper with other interested parties, via the Internet, you may wish to consider joining the National Council for Educational Technology's (NCET) SENCO forum. Over 500 participants currently swap ideas and share their expertise in SEN through this Mailbase service. Details of how to join, free of charge, are available on the NCET's site at **http://www.ncet.org.uk/senco/**.

Abbreviations

DfEE	Department for Education and Employment
EBD	Emotional and Behavioural Difficulties
EDP	Education Development Plan
EP	Educational Psychologist
FE	Further Education
FEFC	Further Education Funding Council
GCSE	General Certificate of Secondary Education
GEST	Grants for Education Support and Training
GNVQ	General National Vocational Qualification
GO	Government Office
HMI	Her Majesty's Inspector
IEP	Individual Education Plan
ICT	Information and Communications Technology
IT	Information Technology
ITT	Initial Teacher Training
LSA	Learning Support Assistant
LEA	Local Education Authority
LMS	Local Management of Schools
NCET	National Council for Educational Technology
NHS	National Health Service
NRA	National Record of Achievement
NVQ	National Vocational Qualification
NQT	Newly Qualified Teacher
OFSTED	Office for Standards in Education
OHMCI	Office of Her Majesty's Chief Inspector
PRU	Pupil Referral Unit
QCA	Qualifications and Curriculum Authority
SEN	Special Educational Needs
SENCO	Special Educational Needs Co-ordinator
TTA	Teacher Training Agency

Printed in the United Kingdom for the Stationery Office Limited
on behalf of the Controller of Her Majesty's Stationery Office
Dd 5067723 10/97, 48003, 22-525, J27368

1

And you run and run
To catch up with the sun
But it is sinking
Racing around to come
Up behind you again.

The sun is the same
(In a relative way)
But you're older
Shorter of breath
And one day
Closer to death